Contents

Introduction

Whitby is one of the most picturesque towns in England. It is an old fishing and whaling port situated on Yorkshire's Heritage Coast where the Esk, through towering cliffs to the east and west, meets the North Sea in a spectacular natural harbour, the largest between the Tyne and the Humber.

The town has a fine mixture of property ranging from the ruins of the great medieval abbey, through to town houses from the same era, Georgian houses, fine Victorian property – especially the unfinished Crescent on the West Cliff – and some interesting modern properties that can be found throughout the town.

Of all the features of Whitby's property that strike a chord with the town's visitors, the red pantile roofs of many of its buildings are, perhaps, the most significant. Much of eastern coastal England's roofs are made of similar materials. Pantiles, from the Dutch *dakpan,* or 'roof pan', were first imported into England from Holland in the late seventeenth century. In Whitby, the tiles appear to glow in the sunlight of summer days and do not retreat, on cold winter days, into the darkness of the heavy grey or green slate roofs of other parts of Yorkshire and the north of England.

The red pantile roofs of Whitby are a stark contrast to the slate tiles often found in Yorkshire.

Pantiles stacked neatly in an alcove in one of Whitby's many yards.

Spectacular as Whitby's location is – with its cliff top buildings, winding streets, ancient street plan and its fascinating harbour – it is not this that attracts visitors to the town. Whitby is a place to escape to: a place in which one can forget the troubles of the present world and seek out solace, not only in a mythical past (something at which Whitby excels) but also in a historic past, one which is deep and enduring.

On the top of the East Cliff, 200 feet above the sea, are the substantial ruins of the church of the Norman Benedictine Abbey of Whitby which was refounded in 1077 on the site of St Hilda's Celtic abbey of AD 657. This was the location for the great Synod of Whitby: the first significant meeting of the early English Church. The meeting impacts on us all, even today, as the Synod of 664 settled the means by which Easter was, and is, determined.

St Hilda's reputation for holiness and wisdom established Whitby as a place of pilgrimage, which extended into the Norman and later medieval periods. It was this that was responsible for the development of the town which grew up, not only under the protection of the monks but also of the east cliff. It was there that the first civil settlement was established and it is in this part of Whitby that many of the town's interesting buildings are located.

However, it was the harbour, protected by the east and west cliffs from the often cruel North Sea, that provided the impetus for Whitby's development as a centre of trade and industry. Whitby, in medieval times, was a small fishing town; small because the town was cut off, by land, from the centres of population that might, otherwise, have provided Whitby its market.

A curious example of a medieval building on Whitby's East Cliff indicates the town's lasting history.

The town's isolated location might have been a problem for others but the men of Whitby were made of sterner stuff. Even in the Middle Ages they were shipping coal from the Tyne to the great abbey that dominated their small community. As other towns and cities along England's east coast grew, it was the descendants of the owners of these Whitby 'colliers', as the coal-carrying vessels were known, who pioneered what became a huge coastal trade in coal.

It is remarkable to record that at one time, though there was no coal to be mined in the Whitby area, there were about 100 Whitby colliers plying the seas between the north-east and carrying coal to the heart of the City of London. The demand for coal was huge, but not only that all of these ships needed to be built and maintained and Whitby men did not commission ships from Newcastle or Sunderland, they built and repaired them themselves, establishing, in the process, a shipbuilding industry which was responsible for some of the most famous ships ever built.

The Whitby of the eighteenth century remained a town of fishermen, 'collier ships' and shipbuilding but another great occupation emerged and it was one in which the people of Whitby excelled: whaling. Numerous Whitby men risked their lives hunting in the North Atlantic and polar regions for whales that were brought back, in large numbers, to Whitby for their blubber and the oil, into which it was converted, for a host of uses.

None of these industries, apart from a little fishing, has lasted into modern times though signs of them all can still be detected in the present town. In fact much of

Above: Whitby's famous yards are little treasures, hidden off the main routes.

Right: Intricate buildings that reflect Whitby's maritime history. This building evokes images of old ships from years gone by.

Whitby's economic past is there to be rediscovered. Much of it dates from the days of self-sufficiency before the coming of the railways, which ended Whitby's landward isolation and opened up the town. Similarly, hints at Whitby's commercial past can be found in the blue plaques of the Civic Society, the curious names of many of the town's streets, and in Whitby's many interesting little buildings.

If you are to enjoy Whitby you have to do so with your eyes wide open. The Whitby of today is an eclectic mixture of all that has been noted so far and its singular, often other-worldly, history. This has inspired writers, from the author most associated with Whitby, Bram Stoker (the creator of Dracula), to Elizabeth Gaskell, Charles Dickens and Lewis Carroll. They, and other more recent writers, not only visited Whitby but they brought their talents to the town, its sea and its countryside, reaching for and writing about that which makes Whitby distinctive, what it is.

We might wonder how many of these writers realised that, when undertaking their works, they were at the very heart of English literature, the place where it all began. It is not generally realised that the oldest poem that can be attributed to an English poet was written in Whitby by Caedmon, a local man, in the eighth century AD.

Whitby is a place of both secrets and surprises and these are what make the town such a pleasure to visit. The visitor never quite knows what will be seen, or heard, next. This is the Whitby we are about to experience. As they say, 'enjoy'.

Roger Frost & Ian Thompson

Whitby entertainment.

1. Historical Whitby

Founding Whitby

Records from the sixth century show that Whitby was probably called Streonaeshalch; which may mean 'fort bay' or 'tower bay', though some think it may simply mean 'Streona's settlement' (a corner of land, or halch, belonging to Streona). If you're thinking to yourself, 'That sounds like Strensall', then you're not far off the mark. Strensall is a village just to the north of York and is probably most famous for the army training camp and firing ranges there at Queen Elizabeth II barracks. So, why is this?

Whitby, the name, was unknown in Anglian times. In fact, it is an Old Norse word: Hwitebi, which means 'white settlement'. However, this name wasn't used until about the twelfth century and by this time a great deal had already taken place.

In the seventh century, Northumbria was divided into two kingdoms: Deira and Bernicia. They were united in AD 604 by Aethelfrith – the first king of Northumbria. This unification was pretty much stable for the era except for a few periods of chaos, particularly during mid-seventh century when Deira was ruled by individual kings. At this time, King Oswui of Bernicia had King Oswine of Deira killed and put in place a new king; Aethelwald, who was to act as a sub-king to Oswui. Unfortunately for Oswui, all did not go to plan and Aethelwald defected to the rival Mercians led by King Penda.

Penda and his allies advanced with a force led by thirty warlords and besieged Oswui's army at Urbs Iudeu. Intent on avoiding a massive battle, Oswiu offered treasure to Penda in exchange for peace at Iudeu. According to the writings of the Venerable Bede, who chronicled these events, Oswui's offers of treasure were rejected by Penda, who remained determined to wipe out Oswui's people 'from the highest to the lowest'.

The Venerable Bede also stated that Oswui's young son Ecgfrith was being held hostage by Penda, and perhaps this formed as part of the deal that saw Penda and his army retreat back to Mercia. While heading back, Penda's army was ambushed by Oswui's forces at the River Winwaed.

Penda and his army would have been in a difficult strategic location along the river during their withdrawal, giving Oswiu a good opportunity to attack, despite the small size of his army. Penda's army was further depleted by the cowardly desertion of Cadafael ap Cynfeddw of Gwynedd (an act that caused him to forever be remembered as 'Cadomedd', or 'Battle-Shirker') and the traitor Aethelwald (who sat out the battle in a safe place to see who the victor would be and, presumably, to realign his loyalties).

During the ferocious battle Penda was decapitated, his remaining troops were defeated and according to Bede 'many more were drowned in the flight than destroyed by the sword' as they tried to cross the river. The battle had taken place during heavy rain and the fast flowing river had become swollen.

St Hilda (614–680) was the founding abbess of the monastery at Whitby.

If you are wondering how this affects Whitby: before the battle, legend stated that Oswiu prayed to God and promised to make his daughter a nun and grant twelve estates for the construction of monasteries if he was victorious. Oswiu was true to his word and gifted the twelve estates: six in Bernicia and six in Deira. He also entered his daughter into a monastery at Heruteu (known today as Hartlepool), which was ruled by Abbess Hilda. Two years later, Hilda founded another monastery at Streonaeshalch.

You will remember that King Oswiu granted land after his great battle with Penda and some say that there was indeed a monastery at Strensall. There has also been speculation that there could have been a twin monastery at Whitby, linked by name in a similar way to Llanthory in the Black Mountains of Wales is twinned with Llanthory (secunda) in Gloucester. Or perhaps in the eighth century when life became a little more heated, the monastery, with links to the increasingly unpopular Oswui, decided to move from the outskirts of York and relocate on the coast of the North Sea, taking the name with it.

Whatever the reason, this was the birth of Whitby and the founding of the abbey which, through time, evolved to become the iconic landmark it is today.

The Great Abbey

The most outstanding building in Whitby is the ruined abbey, which dominates the town from its position high on the East Cliff. The view constitutes one of the great landscape images of Yorkshire and it is famous throughout the world, but it should not be forgotten that the abbey at Whitby was founded for the worship of God.

Whitby Abbey, as it stands today, on the East Cliff.

As we have seen, the abbey reached an early peak in its fame with its very first abbess, St Hilda. In the mid-seventh century it was the location for the first great meeting of the English Church and it has a claim, through Caedmon, to be the birthplace of English literature. In later years the brooding hilltop ruins of the second abbey inspired Bram Stoker to write his novel *Dracula* and writers and artists have followed him with their works.

We will look at them elsewhere in this book, but it is as a monastic institution that we will consider Whitby for now. St Hilda's appointment as founding abbess set the standard for the first incarnation of the monastery. It lasted for 200 years at the end of which the north-east of England was convulsed by the invasions of the Danes, or Vikings as they are sometimes called.

The Danes, like the Anglo-Saxons and the Romans before them, left their mark on this part of the country but, at first, they were the great destroyers of what had been achieved at Whitby and other monasteries in the area. For another 200 years or so the abbey was deserted, destroyed by time and the Danes until a revival took place.

The present abbey ruins date from that revival, which took place in the eleventh century shortly after the Norman Conquest. The story is of a Norman knight who came to England with William the Conqueror. He has come down to us as Reinfrid and he is supposed to have witnessed the king's 'harrying of the north', which was a successful and bloody attempt to put down a rebellion led by some of the last surviving Anglo-Saxon lords.

Reinfrid, moved by what he saw when he was in the north of William's new kingdom, decided to become a monk and entered the abbey at Evesham in Worcestershire. Four years later he travelled with two companions to Jarrow, another great religious centre in the north of England, and when he was there he had a vision to re-establish the great abbey at Whitby.

This could not have been done without the support of a local lord; William de Percy stepped forward and gave property to Reinfrid, who was soon joined by other men. Together they founded, for a second time, an abbey at Whitby. This was in 1076 though, and at first the new Benedictine institution was only a priory. It was not granted abbey status until the early twelfth century.

At this time the earliest abbey buildings had been constructed. The church and some of the monastic buildings date from this period, though some of these were altered, and others were added, in the thirteenth century. In the twelfth century, a leper hospital was constructed at Spittal Bridge, which is on Spittal Beck to the south of Whitby Abbey. Also at this time, the parish church of St Mary was built close to the abbey precinct.

It would be fair to say that the second abbey at Whitby, though its buildings were much more impressive than those of the first, did not reach the high religious standards set by its predecessor. However, the new Whitby Abbey was a very important institution in Whitby and the surrounding countryside. The abbey owned and managed land and property over a wide expanse. It cared for the religious need of the people of the Whitby area through the running of their local churches. The abbey gave employment to many local people and it supported their local crafts and industries.

However, useful and important though it had been, the age of the monasticism came to an end in the sixteenth century. It was on 14 December 1539 that the fate of Whitby Abbey was sealed. The date is significant because it was at this time, at the end of a process instigated by Henry VIII, that Whitby, one of the great houses, was forced into closure.

The process, known as Suppression of the Monasteries, had started in the South of England some years before Henry came to the throne in 1509. In this part of the country the number of novices entering the religious houses started to decline. Others were too small to continue. Some combined with houses of their own order, leaving one open where there may have been three or four before. In other examples, the religious house might close and its assets were sold and converted into cash for other purposes. This is what Cardinal Wolsey planned for his great college at Cambridge, which he planned to name after himself. However, before this was achieved Wolsey failed to get the divorce from Katherine of Aragon that the king had so desired. When the Cardinal fell from power, the king took over the project and King's College, Cambridge, was born.

When Whitby Abbey closed, the buildings were stripped of its lead, glass and valuables. The abbey was left to crumble into the ruin that we know today. The great church at the abbey, though roofless with the glass removed from its windows, was pretty intact until the early eighteenth century, but after that time the rate of decay seems to have increased. A number of surviving images of the abbey show that in the eighty or so years from 1711, the nave, south transept and the west front were all falling. But, the greatest loss was that of the central tower, which fell in 1830.

History, however, had not finished with Whitby Abbey. In December 1914 a German battlecruiser shelled Whitby; the abbey gateway and the west wall of the nave were hit. Further damage was done to the abbey but this time by the locals who, as with others who lived in the shadow of monastic buildings, at times took stones for their own building project and gardens.

The Ministry of Works took over the maintenance of the still substantial remains in 1920 and since that time the abbey has been cared for, most recently by English Heritage. Of course what is left is diminished by what has been lost, but enough survives of Whitby Abbey for the visitor to see that the magnificent ruin it now is was once one of the most beautiful monastic buildings in England.

It is no wonder that people still want to make the journey to this building, situated as it is on the edge of both the North Sea and the North Yorkshire Moors. Many of them choose to get there by means of the 199 steps that lead to the abbey from above the harbour, but when the visitor gets to the site the experience is made all the better by heading for the Visitor Centre. This was built as a private house by the Cholmley family, once the owners of the site, who plundered the ancient abbey for its building materials.

There is no chance of that sort of thing now. Whitby Abbey might not have its ancient role, but it still casts a spell over the thousands of people who make their way to this ancient site, thoughts of Hilda, Caedmon and the great Synod of Whitby on their minds.

How the Abbey Fixed Easter

Have you ever wondered why Easter is never on the same day each year? Christianity in Britain during the seventh century existed in two forms: Ionan and Roman traditions. The Ionan practice was that of the Irish monks of the isle of Iona, and the Roman tradition kept observances according to the customs of Rome.

In the kingdom of Northumbria these two traditions coexisted and each had been encouraged by different royal houses. One of the most controversial differences between the two traditions was the calculation of when Easter would fall. Early Christians had aligned the festival with the Jewish Passover (the fourteenth day of the first lunar month of the Jewish year), which was the day of the crucifixion. However, in AD 325 the First Council of Nicaea ruled that the Jewish calendar was not to be used and that Christians must adopt the practice of celebrating Easter on a Sunday, the day of the resurrection, as was the custom in Rome. Calculating the proper date of Easter involved the use of a lunisolar calendar and this, in turn, led to various calculation tables being developed, resulting in different dates for the celebration of Easter.

In the 660s, the Ionans used a system devised in the third century by Bishop Augustalis that worked to an eighty-four-year cycle. Meanwhile, in Rome, the 532 year tables of Dionysius Exiguus were being utilised.

The ambiguity of Easter's proper date had already resulted in some fractures appearing in the unity of the Northumbrian court: Queen Eanfled of Bernicia observed Easter on a different day than King Oswiu did. This meant that while one royal house enjoyed a period of feasting as they celebrated, the other was still strictly observing Lent. Even so, things seemed to manage without much trouble, until the time of the third Ionan monk elected Bishop of Northumbria, Colman, decided that the conflict required attention and resolution.

To resolve this matter a synod (a gathering to discuss religious doctrine) was convened at Hilda's monastery. This was to be the famous Synod of Whitby and was to have long-lasting consequences for the Christian church. Hilda was a noblewoman of Northumbrian descent and her stance leaned heavily towards supporting the Ionan Easter, advocated by Colman. Oswiu presided over the synod and acted as the final judge. Colman maintained that the Ionan calculation of Easter should be adopted on the grounds that it was the practice of Columba, founder of the Ionan monastic network and a saint of unquestionable holiness. The Roman position was promoted by Alchfrith who was the son of Oswui and the sub-king in Deira. In the early 660s Alchfrith had expelled Ionan monks from the monastery of Ripon and handed it over to the Northumbrian churchman named Wildred, who had recently returned from Rome.

Bede wrote at the time that Wilfrid had argued the Roman position on the grounds that it was the practice in Rome, the place where the apostles St Peter and St Paul had 'lived, taught, suffered, and are buried'; and it was the universal practice of the Church. Columba had done the best he could considering his knowledge, and thus his irregular practice is

The Venerable Bede (673–735) was known as the 'Father of English History' and wrote extensively about the Synod of Whitby

excusable, but the Ionan monks did not have the excuse of ignorance and whatever the case, no one has authority over St Peter.

Oswiu is reported to have then asked both sides if they agreed that St Peter had been given the keys to the kingdom of Heaven by Christ and pronounced to be 'the rock' on which the church would be built. Both sides of the synod were in agreement with this and it was left for Oswiu to judge in favour of 'the holder of the keys' – St Peter. The Roman practice was therefore adopted, bringing the Northumbrian church into the mainstream of Roman culture and securing Easter ever since.

The Abbey at War

Between the years AD 867 and 870 the abbey first came under attack from Vikings, led by the fierce Ingwar and Ubba. The two Danes rampaged through England, taking York and defeating all resistance. By 870 the abbey lay in ruins and the Vikings had a new name for the place. In Old Norse it was 'Prestebi' meaning 'Settlement of Priests'.

After the Norman Conquest, William De Percy (the first baron of Topcliffe) was granted land in Yorkshire, including the area known as Prestebi. In 1079 William donated this land to an order of Benedictine monks in order to allow them to found a monastery to St Peter and St Hilda. William also gifted land for what was to become the town of Whitby and many surrounding churches. The abbey is the one that you can see today in Whitby and it survived until December 1539 when it fell under Henry VIII's Dissolution of the Monasteries.

The abbey rested for nearly 400 years, slowly falling into ruin, but it remained a prominent landmark for shipping and other travellers. It wasn't until 1914 that the abbey was violated again by a sea bombardment by the German battle cruisers *Von der Tann* and *Derfflinger*. It was the latter ship's first combat raid in a daring attack to draw out the Grand Fleet into a sea battle where the Royal Navy ships could be defeated.

The plan almost worked, except for the fact that the British knew something was in the planning. They had been privy to German codebooks, captured by the Russians four months previously, and their messages had been intercepted and decoded. Lying in wait for the German Navy was a taskforce led by Vice Admiral David Beatty.

Von der Tann and *Derfflinger* were part of a group that had been tasked to bombard Hartlepool, Whitby, and Scarborough. That group had inadvertently split from a larger one that had ceased the operation for fear of being torpedoed by the British. The rogue group continued with their mission, unaware that the rest of the fleet had retreated, and on the night of 15 December 1914, shells intended for the signal post on Whitby's cliff top rained down and badly damaged the abbey.

The next morning this raiding party had rejoined the battle group and steamed away towards Vice Admiral Beatty's ambush. Due to a communication breakdown, the German ships were able to avoid any conflict and escaped. Both the *Von der Tann* and the *Derfflinger* survived the war, but were scuttled at Scapa Flow in 1919.

This shows that the town of Whitby and its abbey have had a turbulent past, which is in stark contrast to the tranquil fishing port that we know and love today. But, as you would expect from a town with such a rich history, there's going to be a few tales to tell...

German battlecruiser, the *Derfflinger*.

German battlecruiser, the *Von der Tann*.

Situated on the West Cliff, this recreation of a shelled home reminds visitors of the German bombardment during the First World War.

The Elephants Who Hated the Sand

There is an interesting picture of two elephants on the beach at Whitby, and an even more interesting tale that goes along with it.

Between Sandsend and Whitby there is a lonely old house by the side of the road. It used to be a toll house and in 1925 it collected its final fee and raised the barrier for the last time. Today it is a private home and the passing motorist probably pays it little, or no, attention, unaware that it was built under the instructions of an Indian maharajah in the 1860s.

Born in September 1838, Duleep Singh was the last maharajah of the Sikh Empire. He was catapulted into this position shortly after his fifth birthday when his four predecessors were assassinated. Clearly, a five year old child would not be able to rule an empire and so his mother ruled in his place as regent. This lasted for three years until the First Anglo–Sikh war when she was deposed and replaced by British resident.

Young Duleep was separated from his mother, and after three years he was sent to Fatehgarh in the Uttar Pradesh region of India where he was placed in the care of Dr John Login. Strict instructions were provided for the young prince about who he could and

A curious sight on Whitby's beach – two elephants. But where did they come from?

The old toll house on the Whitby to Sandsend Road.

could not interact with and according to British policy at the time, he was to be anglicised 'in every possible way'.

Dr Login was a highly devout Christian and he made sure that his young charge was exposed to Christianity as much as possible. In order to emphasise this he provided Duleep with his two closest friends, who both happened to be English Anglican missionaries. By the time he was fifteen years old, the maharajah had converted to Christianity.

In 1854 Duleep was exiled to Britain, where he soon became a sensation within the royal household. He was a frequent guest of Queen Victoria and Prince Albert and was often sketched while playing with the royal children.

In the mid-1850s he relocated to Scotland, leasing property at Auchlyne. While there, Duleep was renowned for his lavish lifestyle and would often dress in Highland costume and stalk the moors dressed as a Scottish laird while on one of his many shooting parties.

Then, in 1858, Duleep returned to England and took out a lease on Mulgrave Castle, just outside of Whitby. What you may not know is that the castle that stands today is actually the third castle built on that site.

The first castle was constructed by Wada, a sixth-century Swedish ruler of a district known as Halsingland. The second castle was built several hundred years later by Nigel Fossard, who acquired the estate following the Norman Conquest. He built an immense stronghold protected by a moat and drawbridge. Unfortunately, the ground on which he built the castle was uneven, causing the walls to bow out so that they required support from large buttresses. Over time the castle passed through various different families and its last role was as a Royalist garrison during the English Civil War. In 1647 it was destroyed by Parliamentary forces. The ruins can still be visited today.

The current castle is actually a castellated mansion that was ordered by Catherine Darnley, the wife of John Sheffield, 1st Duke of Buckingham and Normanby. Catherine's daughter married into the Phipps family and since 1718 until the present day, the Phipps' have owned Mulgrave Castle and its estate.

It would appear that Duleep lost none of his extravagance while he was at Mulgrave: it's rumoured that he and his retinue would travel from the castle into Whitby on the backs of elephants. At the time they would walk along the beach, but the maharajah, it is said, became increasingly worried about his elephants. They seemed to dislike getting sand between their toes, which prompted Duleep into action.

Duleep ordered that a road be constructed between Sandsend and Whitby in order to make the journey more pleasurable for his elephants. The completed road no doubt served its purpose and also shortened the journey time between the towns.

All of this seems quite a romantic tale, but sadly, even though we know that he ordered the building of the road, there is no evidence that Duleep Singh ever kept elephants at Musgrave Castle or rode them into Whitby. But what of that curious picture of the elephants on the beach underneath the battery at Whitby? It is highly likely that they were from a circus that was visiting the town.

And what happened to Duleep? Sadly his fortunes turned and he ended up penniless. He died in a hotel in Paris in 1893 of an epileptic fit.

Above: Was this road built to protect the elephants from getting sand between their toes?

Left: The Maharajah of Mulgrave Castle – Duleep Singh.

Did you know?
The famous Koh i Noor diamond was given to Queen Victoria by Duleep Singh.

The Fossil Coast

As the weather and rough seas crash against the steep cliffs around Whitby it is almost inevitable that, at some point, part of that cliff face will come crashing down onto the beach below. And when it does, it leaves behind some of the most exciting treasures that provide scientists with an insight into a lost world, millions of years old.

At the beginning of the twenty-first century, a forensic scientist and amateur geologist named Alan Gurr was on a field trip with his friend, Professor Phil Manning, and the Yorkshire Geological Society at Whitby, where they were exploring the shore between Whitby and Scarborough. Professor Manning was explaining how there had been fossilised dinosaur tracks found in that area which meant that, inevitably, dinosaur bones should be discoverable. Alan Gurr asked his friend what these bones would look like and the Professor told him that they should look for rocks with speckles of white calcite in a crunchy, bar structure. Alan pointed to a boulder behind him and said 'you mean a bit like that?'

What Alan had just discovered was to become, fifteen years later, the oldest dinosaur bone ever found in Britain. The 15 kilogram vertebrae is believed to be 176 million years old and has been attributed to a sauropod – a type of long-necked and long-tailed dinosaur similar to a brontosaurus.

At the beginning of the nineteenth century, geology was a new science and it led to many theories about the age of the Earth. It was thought that the world was anywhere between hundreds of thousands of years old, to billions of years old (it is now generally accepted that the world is about two billion years old). Part of this new geological science postulated that fossils may be the remains of once living animals and it led to the realisation that

The cliffs beneath Whitby Abbey are rich in fossils.

Whitby has a long history of trade in fossils dug from the cliffs. Today visitors can still buy a range of fossils in the town.

the Earth was composed of many different layers, each with their corresponding place in time. Through this study many fossils were found, including ammonites, plants, and even the large skeletons of marine reptiles on the coast near Whitby. It is generally thought that one of the earliest recorded discoveries of a fossil having been discovered in this area was in 1758, when a skeleton of a prehistoric crocodile was uncovered during an operation to extract alum from the surrounding rocks. It was extracted by Captain William Chapman, named *Teleosaurus chapmani*, and later donated to the British Museum.

It turned out that there was a market in these large fossils and local quarrymen would often sell them as curiosities, making a handsome profit. In order to save them the Reverend George Young helped to establish the Whitby Literary and Philosophical Society and ultimately founded the Whitby Museum, where many examples of local fossils can be seen today.

The smaller fossils have also played a large part in the history of Whitby. In the poem *Marmion, A Tale of Flodden Field* by Sir Walter Scott it says:

> How of a thousand snakes, each one
> Was changed into a coil of stone,
> When holy Hilda prayed.

This passage is a reference to an ancient legend where St Hilda, searching for a site to build her abbey, found a field that was infested with snakes. She began to pray and

The legend of St Hilda turning snakes to stone has long been used to explain the proliferation of ammonite fossils in the area.

according to legend the snakes fell from the cliff, curled up and were petrified into stone. It was a handy way to explain the discovery of these thousands of strange coiled stones on the beaches at Whitby.

It was common practice for industrious entrepreneurs to carve snake heads onto the fossils and sell them as 'snakestones'. Today, we recognise them as the fossilised remains of the ammonite *Hildoceras*, a genus named after St Hilda in 1876. In fact, this legend is immortalised in the arms of Whitby Town Council, which features three green ammonites with snake's heads.

Whitby is an excellent place to come fossil hunting and guides can be obtained to assist the casual visitor on how to go about it. While actually hunting for fossils is not inherently dangerous, the locations where the fossils may be found are. Most of the fossils come about because of the deterioration of the cliffs and rock fall is a constant danger, as are the slippery rocks of the shoreline and the threat of the incoming tide, but with the correct, sensible precautions, a great deal of fun can be had.

It is possible, with some advice and luck, to spot the fossilised footprints of dinosaurs on those shale shores. In fact, while researching this chapter one of the authors decided to take a quick excursion from Tate Hill Sands onto the beach beneath the cliffs to look for fossils. As I picked my way across the boulders I had not gone more than five metres from the East pier when, beneath their feet was the fossil of a dinosaur's footprint!

It was the author's first attempt at fossil hunting, and what a find! We would encourage anyone to have a search using one of the many guidebooks available. Who knows, you may even discover a previously unknown species of dinosaur!

Fossil hunting at the foot of Whitby's cliffs remains a popular pastime.

Whitby's fossils.

An exciting find! A three-toed dinosaur footprint.

Victoria's Jewellery

It is not just dinosaurs and ammonites that have made Whitby famous in the world of fossils. Another fossil helped bolster the fortunes of this great town due to a fashionable piece of jewellery worn by Queen Victoria.

Whitby jet is a black substance that is the fossilised wood of a type of Jurassic plant similar to the 'monkey puzzle tree' and is approximately 182 million years old. Jet exists all over the globe and what is found in Whitby is believed by many to be the best example in the world, probably because of the compression on the rotten remains and the salty water.

In the Jurassic period, Whitby and the rest of the Yorkshire coast would have started off as the bottom of a warm tropical sea before, over hundreds of thousands of years, becoming a marshy river delta, dotted with swamps and lagoons.

As time progressed and the sea receded, the cliffs surrendered their deposits onto the beaches and jet was exposed to the world.

There is evidence of it having been used in the Neolithic period and the Bronze Age, where it became used for necklace beads. The Romans later adopted jet as a fashion item; many items can be seen today in the Yorkshire Museum. Its popularity declined and it wasn't until the Victorian era when it took off again.

When Queen Victoria's husband, Prince Albert, died in 1861 she took to wearing black to show that she was in mourning. The queen had jewellery made from Whitby jet and it was an instant sensation with the public who sought to imitate her look.

It was extravagant yet remained modest in appearance and ever since Whitby is the place to go to for quality jet jewellery. Many shops in Whitby sell these decorative items and perhaps now you'll be tempted to take away, as a souvenir of your visit, a delicate piece of jewellery that has, quite literally, taken millions of years to produce.

Queen Victoria popularised the wearing of jet jewellery after the death of Prince Albert.

Above: A traditional Victorian jet works at Tate Hill in Whitby.

Below: Jet workshops still operate today, providing the visitor an opportunity to purchase jewellery.

2. Mysterious Whitby

The World's Most Famous Vampire

Dracula. He needs no further introduction. Since Bram Stoker's epic novel was published in 1897, it has never been out of print.

More than 200 films have been made about Dracula and over 650 have a reference to him. Numerous 'sequel' novels have been written, plays continue to appear on stage, vampire literature is inspired by him, and his iconic image adorns supermarket shelves and toy shops across the world close to Halloween. Without a doubt, Dracula is the most famous monster in the world, but what has any of that got to do with Whitby?

Bram Stoker was born in Dublin in 1847, a sickly child who remained bedridden for many years. His mother would tell him ghost stories to keep him entertained, which at that time were incredibly popular.

The cover of the first edition of *Dracula* by Bram Stoker.

Bram Stoker, author of *Dracula*, was a regular holidaymaker in Whitby.

It was here that he wrote parts of his famous novel.

Stoker went on to become a successful university student and later a qualified barrister, but gave it all up to manage Sir Henry Irving's Lyceum Theatre in London where he remained until Sir Henry's death in 1905.

In 1878, Stoker left Dublin and married the on-off sweetheart of Oscar Wilde, Florence Balcombe, and a year later their son Noel was born. In August 1890, the Stokers went on holiday to Whitby and chose to stay at No. 6 Royal Crescent.

At that time, Whitby was one of the most popular tourist destinations in the country. It was still a working port but the beautiful views and relative isolation from the rush and the whirl of city life made it a relaxing retreat.

A plaque marks the guest house where Bram Stoker stayed in Whitby.

The enchanting graveyard of St Mary's Church, which features in *Dracula.*

During his holiday in Whitby, Bram Stoker made many notes that made their way into the text of *Dracula* in the form of observations made by Mina Murray, one of his key characters. His favourite place to sit and plot his story was actually in the churchyard on the East Cliff, looking out to sea. This seat became the 'suicide seat' where Mina would rest and the location where her friend Lucy is first attacked by Dracula.

What is not as well known is that Stoker also chatted with local fishermen and the coastguard and heard some extraordinary tales, such as the wrecking of the *Dmitry,* which occurred five years earlier. The *Dmitry* was a Russian ship from the port of Narva that dramatically ran aground during a storm on Tate Hill Sands at the foot of the East Cliff. It was carrying a cargo of silver sand.

The story of this wreck obviously impressed him and became part of his story. Stoker renamed the ship *Demeter* and it became the ship that brought Dracula to England, running aground on Tate Hill Sands. In the story, like its real-life inspiration, the *Demeter* carries a cargo of silver sand and boxes of earth. Its home port was Varna.

Tate Hill Sands – the beach where Dracula's ship, the *Demeter*, ran aground bringing the vampire to England.

On Friday 8 August 1890, Stoker visited the Whitby Public Lending Library (now the Quayside fish and chip restaurant) and read a book called *An Account of the Principalities of Wallachia and Moldavia* by William Wilkinson. While reading this book, Stoker found a reference to a tyrannical Eastern European prince with a penchant for impaling his enemies on large wooden stakes, and other acts of sadism. This man was Vlad Tepes. To his friends and enemies, he was called Dracula, meaning 'The Son of the Dragon'.

It is likely that Stoker wrote his Whitby sections of the book first, followed by the Carpathian chapters, and finally the London portions of the book. The Whitby sections are, perhaps, the most exciting part of the book and feature Dracula's arrival to the town and the attack on his first victim. It is clear to see from Stoker's writing that Whitby made a definite impression on him and he could not help but weave local legends and mythology into his fantastic tale.

The story tells us that during a violent storm the *Demeter*, piloted by the dead captain, runs aground at Tate Hill Sands. As soon as the ship hits the beach a huge black dog is seen to leap from the ship and escapes into the town. Taking their holiday in Whitby at this time are two friends, Mina Murray and Lucy Westenra. Lucy is prone to sleepwalking and one night she walks to the graveyard near Whitby Abbey. Mina makes a midnight dash through the town and finds Lucy at their favourite seat in the graveyard. Lucy later died and then becomes the first of Dracula's victims.

Whitby is rarely mentioned in the many Dracula films and this is a real shame. If it had not been for that holiday in August 1890 then there is every chance that *Dracula* would not have been the success that it was.

Above: Whitby by night – a view unchanged since Bram Stoker's time.

Right: The Dracula Experience on Marine Parade tells Dracula's story.

Many of the locations mentioned in the story can be visited today and you would be pleasantly surprised to notice that very little of Whitby has changed since Bram Stoker took up his pen and began writing the most famous horror story of all time in the town that can honestly claim to be the birthplace of the character Dracula.

The Hand of Glory

Take the right or left hand of a felon who is hanging from a gibbet beside a highway; wrap it in part of a funeral pall and so wrapped squeeze it well. Then put it into an earthenware vessel with zimat, nitre, salt and long peppers, the whole well powdered. Leave it in this vessel for a fortnight, then take it out and expose it to full sunlight during the dog-days until it becomes quite dry. If the sun is not strong enough put it in an oven with fern and vervain. Next make a kind of candle from the fat of a gibbeted felon, virgin wax, sesame, and ponie, and use the Hand of Glory as a candlestick to hold this candle when lighted, and then those in every place into which you go with this baneful instrument shall remain motionless.

Petit Albert, 1722

These dreadful instructions were written in 1722 in the *Petit Albert* – a magical textbook that had been inspired by the studies and writings of Saint Albertus Magnus of Cologne.

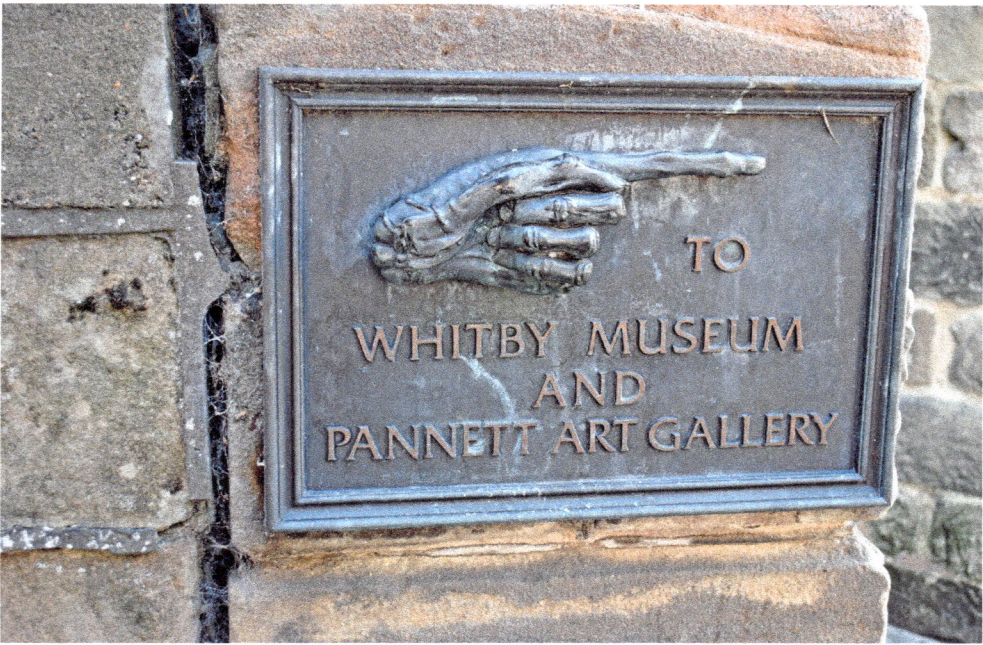

The Hand of Glory points the way to the museum.

Saint Albertus died in 1280 and, as such, there are no definitive records to directly attribute his work to the *Petit Albert*, but the esoteric grimoire was a public sensation when it was published because of its sinister and forbidden content.

What the book tells us is how to make a 'Hand of Glory' which is, quite simply, the dried and preserved hand of a hanged man. If it comes from a murderer then, ideally, you should select the hand that committed the murder. This dried hand, when combined with a candle made from the fat of the hand's donor, became a powerful magical tool. The candle would be placed into the hand with the fingers curled around it. Anyone in the vicinity of this fiendish device (with the exception of the holder) would become unable to move, sleeping a deep and unnatural sleep. The Hand of Glory was the perfect tool for any burglar.

The *Petit Albert*, while providing the recipe for creating the Hand of Glory, also provided a countermeasure. If you wish to protect your house from intruders then you should follow this advice:

> The Hand of Glory would become ineffective, and thieves would not be able to utilize it, if you were to rub the threshold or other parts of the house by which they may enter with an unguent composed of the gall of a black cat, the fat of a white hen, and the blood of the screech-owl; this substance must be compounded during the dog-days.
>
> *Petit Albert*, 1722

The myths and legends concerning the Hand of Glory have grabbed the imagination of generations of people for its element of gory detail. Many other stories survive in the

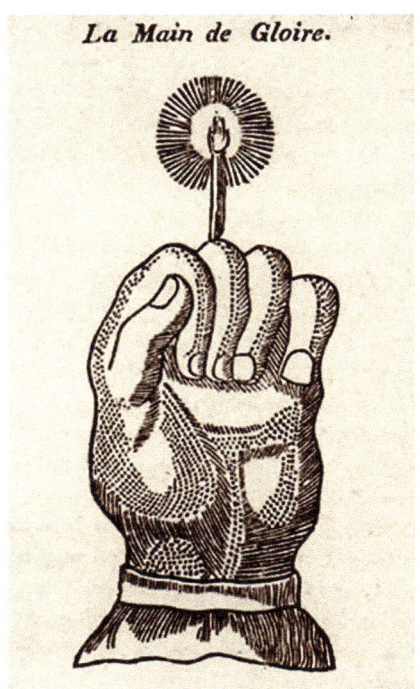

A woodcut of a Hand of Glory shows how it was used to hold a candle.

folklore of this country and abroad that show the benefits that the hand of an executed criminal or drowned person can give.

Most of the hands were used to cure an illness, specifically goitre. This is a swelling of the thyroid gland in your neck, usually the result of an iodine deficiency and so it was relatively common in earlier times. Without knowledge of the cause, it would be impossible to cure. In some cases, the afflicted person was to visit the corpse alone and place the lifeless hand on the growth. Sometimes, the hand was preserved and kept so that it could be used repeatedly. Then, the hand would be passed seven or nine times over the swelling or growth.

Not all of the myths specified the use of a convicted and executed criminal's hand. It was believed that those who had died before they would have done so naturally, could still have life-giving forces in their bodies until the end of what would have been their normal lifespan. This takes folk medicine into the realms of magic and has to be seen in historical context. Many people would go to a wise woman for her knowledge of folk medicine, whereby she used plants to cure an illness or give relief. However, there were many diseases with no cure and so other means were sought to give respite to the sufferer, hence the preserved hand.

Whitby Museum's hand was discovered in the parish of Danby, on the North York Moors, in the early twentieth century. It was given to Joseph Ford, a mason in the village, who was interested in local history and legends. He had heard many legends about the Hand of Glory, and the criminal uses made of it when shaped to hold a candle, and so he kept it. The medical uses are less well-known but this aspect is equally interesting. As this hand was found built into a cottage, it suggests that the owner thought it would continue

Whitby Museum – home of the Hand of Glory.

to offer magical cures as he or she passed by it. The Hand of Glory you can see today came to the museum in 1935.

The hand is on display at Whitby Museum in Pannett Park and is thought to be the only one surviving.

I have said that this is the only known Hand of Glory in existence, but one was believed to have been found in Walsall in the Midlands in the late nineteenth century when a local pub, the White Hart, was being refurbished. As workmen were renovating an attic chimney they discovered, to their horror, a severed child's arm – perfectly preserved.

According to the Walsall Museum, it was first thought to be a Hand of Glory but, as it later transpired, it was a medical exhibit. It was a surgically removed child's arm that had been preserved with formalin.

Did you know?
The candle held by a Hand of Glory could only be extinguished with milk. Any other liquid thrown over it would cause it burn much brighter.

Ghosts and Legends

A place as steeped in history as Whitby is bound to have a number of myths and legends surrounding it, and we want to share with you some of those tales.

From the East Pier it is possible to watch the sun rise from behind the abbey and set behind the headland to our left. It is a strange phenomenon as the sun almost appears to be travelling from south to north, not east to west as it should. And it is from this vantage point that we should look out to the two lighthouses on both the East and West Pier.

The West Pier lighthouse, the taller of the two, was run by a lighthouse keeper. With so many ships wrecked off the shore of this great town, we would expect to find a lighthouse to keep seafarers safe and it was often the duty of the lighthouse keeper to ensure that the ships passed by safe in the stormy nights.

The two lighthouses at Whitby harbour. The taller of the lighthouses is said to be haunted by the ghost of a lighthouse keeper.

One particular night a terrible storm howled around Whitby, making everyone stay safely inside their homes. Rain lashed at the windows and the wind howled around the chimney pots. Thunder crashed, rattling tiles and lightning forked across the night sky. The lighthouse keeper at that time knew that he had to make sure that the great light on top was maintained and he set out for the tower on the West Pier.

By the time he reached the door at the base of the lighthouse he was soaked to the skin, but he diligently made his way up the narrow stone stairs that curved round and round. He made it to the top of the tower and lit the light. The reflectors rotated and the beam of brilliant white light cut through the storm.

With his job done, the lighthouse keeper turned to head back down the stairs. As he started his descent he slipped. His rain-sodden clothes had dripped onto the steps and caused them to become slippery. The lighthouse keeper tumbled down the stairs, his momentum causing him to gather speed and he continued to fall until the door of the lighthouse stopped him, dead. His neck was broken.

If you are brave enough, you could visit the lighthouse on a stormy night and see if you can catch sight of the determined keeper as he performs his duty beyond the grave.

From here you can look up towards Whitby Abbey and imagine how grand it would have looked before it was destroyed. It is said that the abbey had the most musical bells in the area, if not the world, and they were the envy of many.

Our next legend takes us to years gone by when an unknown freebooter decided to take advantage of those bells and claim them as their own. This pirate organised a raiding party and set sail for Whitby where they landed and began their assault on the abbey.

The West Pier lighthouse.

The plunderers were a sizeable force and succeeded in extracting the bells from the abbey and set sail with their prize, returning to wherever it was that they had come.

As they turned their ship south they struck the prominent rock of Black Nab and, weighted down by the Abbey Bells, sunk to the bottom of the North Sea.

It is said that if you are to visit Black Nab at Halloween and call out the name of your most loved one in the middle of the dark night, you will hear their name echoing back at you on the sea breeze, accompanied by the wedding chimes of the sunken abbey bells.

We stay with a musical theme as we travel a moderate distance from Whitby, to the market town of Knaresborough where, in 1717, John Metcalfe was born. At the age of six years old he lost his sight after contracting smallpox. In order to make sure he would still be able to make an income, he was given lessons to teach him how to play the violin; he became a highly accomplished player and began to earn money as a travelling entertainer.

Refusing to allow his blindness to hold him back, John (or 'Blind Jack' as he became known) took up swimming, diving, playing cards, gambling, and cock fighting. He was also quite popular with the ladies and in 1739 he befriended Dorothy Benson, the daughter of the landlord of the Granby Inn in Harrogate.

He continued his womanising and eventually made another woman pregnant. Dorothy stood by Jack and begged him not to marry the woman. Jack decided that he should make himself scarce and he left for the North Sea coast, lodging with his aunt in Whitby.

He continued to find work playing his violin until he received word that his beloved Dorothy was to be married to a shoemaker. He returned to her and they eloped. Their marriage produced four children. Sadly, Dorothy died in 1778.

Blind Jack of Knaresborough.

Blind Jack became an astute businessman and worked as a carrier of goods before taking advantage of a 1765 Act of Parliament that permitted the building of turnpike roads. At that time there were very few skilled road builders but Blind Jack, drawing on his considerable experience as a carrier, set about building roads. He was to build approximately 180 miles of roads in Yorkshire, Lancashire, Cheshire, and Derbyshire; he impressed his peers when he devised a way of laying roads over boggy land using foundations made of bundles of heather and gorse.

The building of great canals across Britain began to cut into his profits: water had replaced road as the primary means of transport. Blind Jack retired to Spofforth where he lived with his daughter and her husband until his death in 1810.

In spite of his blindness, he was regarded as one of the greatest road engineers of the Industrial Revolution. Many of the roads he built continue to be some of the busiest routes in the North of England. Jack certainly left his mark, but he also left a lasting legacy in Whitby.

At the end of Grape Lane on the eastern side of Whitby is a reserved car park, built sometime in the 1950s. Prior to this it was site of the Tiger Inn, which could be accessed by a narrow alley known as Cockpit Yard. This dim passage would open into a square yard that derived its name from the Cock Pit – the place where cockfighting would take place.

When Cockpit Yard still stood, residents would report that during the night they were woken by the sound of a violin being played in the yard. When they looked out of the

Tin Ghaut car park on the site of Cockpit Yard where the ghost of Blind Jack would play his fiddle.

window they saw a ghostly figure with bandages over his eyes playing the fiddle. This apparition would remain in view until some brave soul would venture into the yard to investigate causing the spirit to vanish.

Was this the ghost of Blind Jack? We shall never know, but this is just one of many mysteries that can be found among the streets of Whitby.

Not far from the old site of the Tiger Inn is Grape Lane, where Captain Cook once lodged when he was an apprentice. Grape Lane can still be visited today; it is a quaint, curving street with a small number of shops and excellent restaurants on it.

It's likely that it would have been a much less reputable place, providing entertainment for many of the sailors in the town. Grape Lane was very probably once known as

Grape Lane.

St Mary's churchyard.

'Grope Lane', a common name for a thoroughfare that reflected the main profession of that locality, in this case – prostitution. In time, the name of the lane was changed to reflect the moral attitudes of the eighteenth and nineteenth centuries, and so Grope Lane became Grape Lane.

No. 17a Grape Lane was once home to the Whitby Photographic Archives. There have been reports of an old sailor's ghost walking along a corridor in the cellar of this old house. In its time, No. 17a has been a bank and even a seaman's hospital. Could this be the ghost of some poor unfortunate sailor who died in that old hospital?

Staying with our ghostly seafarers, there is a legend within Whitby that a sailor from the town who perished would be visited in his grave a few days later. On the third night after their funeral, a ghostly coach pulled by a number of headless horses was said would thunder towards the cemetery at St Mary's church.

On board the coach would be a group of skeletal sailors who'd come to pay their respects to their colleague. The coach would then make three laps of the grave, which would cause the ghost to leap from it and join the other spectres before disappearing into the night.

This fearful tale may have its origins in a much more real setting. It was not uncommon for smugglers to use ghost stories to cover up their activities and keep witnesses away from their misdeeds. The coffin of a sailor made an excellent place to hide smuggled goods and it could easily be recovered after the funeral.

There are accounts of smugglers in Dorset who actually painted their horses white (except for the heads) and hung lanterns about the coach to give the impression of glowing phantom carriage. It would have been simple for a gang of roguish smugglers to recount some terrifying tale (which would soon spread through the superstitious townsfolk) before adopting fearsome costumes and undertaking the recovery of their booty. Anyone who happened to see them would, no doubt, be terrified by the sight of a group of reanimated corpses digging up a grave to collect the latest member of their ranks. Talk about hiding in plain sight!

The Old Smuggler café on Baxtergate dates as far back as 1401 and was once called The Old Ship Launch Inn. The Old Smuggler, as its name suggests, had a long involvement in smuggling; rumour has it that it stands on the site of a smuggling tunnel which leads to another nearby pub – the Station Inn. Contraband would arrive at one of these two pubs and then transported, via the tunnel, to be picked up. This would ensure that none of the smuggled goods would be seized by the customs officials of Whitby.

Just outside of the Old Smuggler is a carved wooden figure, believed to be part of a captured French smuggling vessel, although the facts are unknown. This still lends a mysterious air to the place; you would fully expect the inn to have its own resident ghost and indeed it does. However, the ghost of the Old Smuggler Inn is not a visual apparition but more of an odd presence that announces itself by giving people a gentle push.

Not far from the Old Smuggler Inn is Pannet Park which, you may remember, is home to the museum and the grisly Hand of Glory. Within the park, and indeed around Whitby, there used to be many arches made from the jawbones of whales. These were a link to the massive whaling industry that used to support Whitby. Whaling was a dangerous

The curious wooden figurehead outside of the Smugglers Inn.

A wooden Whalebone Arch situated in Pannet Park, where the ghost of a young boy has been seen crying.

occupation with terribly long periods spent away from home in rough Arctic seas and the loss of sailors and even ships was commonplace.

Where one of these whalebone arches once stood there is a tale of a young boy who used to appear next to it. People who witnessed this sight reported that the boy seemed distressed and was crying uncontrollably. No one knows who this boy is but it has been speculated that it is the ghost of a child who served as the cabin boy on a whaling ship but tragically never returned home.

Is this little boy one of these poor souls who may have drowned, frozen to death in the ship's rigging, or been killed due to the ship becoming trapped in the Arctic ice for weeks on end? For when food supplies ran short, dogs, rats, and possibly even the cabin boys, would have been used as a means of preventing starvation.

In the famous trial of Dudley and Stevens in 1884, three sailors and a cabin boy had been shipwrecked and cast adrift in a small boat without provisions. To save themselves, the sailors killed and ate the cabin boy. Later, they were convicted of murder, despite a defence plea that it was a necessity.

It is said that when the whalebone arch in Pannet Park was removed, the ghost of the young boy disappeared.

As we leave Pannet Park and head up Stakesby Road we will soon reach the junction with Love Lane. Here you will find a roughly carved piece of stone which takes the form of a seat. This is Whitby's Wishing Chair. According to legend, a person should sit in the chair, close their eyes and make a wish. If the wish is reasonable and (this is the important part), they tell no other person of their wish, then it will be granted.

The Wishing Chair – any reasonable wishes granted!

When a sea mist rolls in, Whitby takes on a mysterious feel.

I'm sure at this point you may be tempted to take a quick glance around you to see if anyone is watching and, upon seeing that the coast is clear, squeeze into that narrow little chair, close your eyes and make your wish, but I may have to disappoint you. The Wishing Chair is not a magical device but is in actual fact the remains of an old Celtic cross. The base stone would have had a socket carved out of it in which the cross would have been inserted. What we see here is what remains of that socket stone, with one of the sides long broken off. But there's no harm in seeing if the old legend is actually true, is there?

We've only shared with you a very small number of the myths and legends that give Whitby its mysterious appeal; there are many more intriguing tales to discover and the best way to do that would be to take one of the many ghost walks that run most nights from various locations within the town. It is a pleasure to enjoy these evening walks, listening to the guide's exciting and interesting tales, while allowing your mind to wander, picturing times gone by and being wrapped in a light sea mist that only adds to the eerie atmosphere.

Pushing Up Daisies

If you feel up to the challenge, climbing the 199 steps to St Mary's churchyard is definitely worth it. In years gone by the cemetery was much bigger than it is now: erosion and landslides have taken their toll and many graves have been lost as the cliff recedes, leaving a grisly display of coffins poking out of the side of the hill. However, these are quickly and efficiently removed for the sake of dignity.

In spite of this, many fascinating memorials remain; you can still see the gravestone remembering the victims of the 1861 lifeboat disaster propped against the church, saved from falling from the fast eroding clifftop.

Tourists begin their climb up the 199 steps to St Mary's churchyard.

Many visitors to Whitby will climb the steps to visit this graveyard with the sole intention of finding Dracula's grave, but putting that character to one side you will find that this beautiful churchyard offers many more surprises. The first, however, you would have passed without realising it...

As you climb up the twisting stone steps, counting them as you go to ensure that there is, indeed, 199, you would have noticed that there are a number of benches set on large flat areas at intervals. These benches are truly a wonderful place to sit and catch your breath while you watch the harbour or admire the red roofs of Whitby, but they were never designed to provide a place of rest for tourists. Instead, they were constructed to act as 'coffin rests' for weary pall-bearers as they carried the coffins to the graveyard.

What is not commonly known is that St Mary's churchyard is the resting place of two popular childhood characters: Tom Thumb and Humpty Dumpty. Their graves can be discovered towards the back of the church in a small area bordered with a low iron fence.

Between two tall graves, side by side, is a tiny headstone, believed by many Whitby children to be Tom Thumb's last resting place. In reality it is probably the grave of an infant between his two parents. Sadly, the inscriptions have worn away, but you may be able to make out the letters 'I' and 'W' carved on the tiny headstone. The headstone to the left marks the grave of Isaac Woodhouse. Is the smaller grave that of his son or daughter?

Just to the left is a large oval gravestone, believed to hold the shattered pieces of the nursery rhyme character Humpty Dumpty. The sandstone has been weathered to the point where nothing more can be read of the grave.

Not a bench to rest your legs, but a place for resting a coffin.

The grave of Tom Thumb.

Humpty Dumpty's grave.

It is easy to believe that it could actually be the grave of Humpty Dumpty. The nursery rhyme character was never an anthropomorphic egg, but was an infamous cannon that was perched atop a great defensive wall. It was dislodged in battle and came crashing down; the cast metal shattered on impact and destroyed the weapon permanently.

Staying in this enclosed section of the graveyard, a fascinating discovery awaits you in a small alcove at the end of a flagged path. You will find a large, engraved, slab set into the alcove above an old and weathered tomb. The slab has the original inscription from the tomb carved on it:

Here lies the bodies of Francis Huntrodds and his wife Mary who were both born on the same day of the week month and year September ye 19th 1600 married on the day of their birth and after having had 12 children born to them died aged 80 years on the same day of the year they were born ye September 19th 1680 the one not above five hours before ye other.

Husband and wife that did 12 children bare, dyed the same day alike both aged were bout 80 years they lived did part (even on the marriage day) each tender heart so fit a match surely could never be both in their lives and in their deaths agree.

St Mary's churchyard has not given up all of its secrets yet. As you retreat from the Huntrodds' grave, there are more mysteries all around you etched in stone. As you would expect of a town with a rich seafaring history, many stones honour those who lost their lives at sea. But this graveyard also continues to provide little quirks that add to the mystery of the place. For example, local tales speak of a grave that bore the

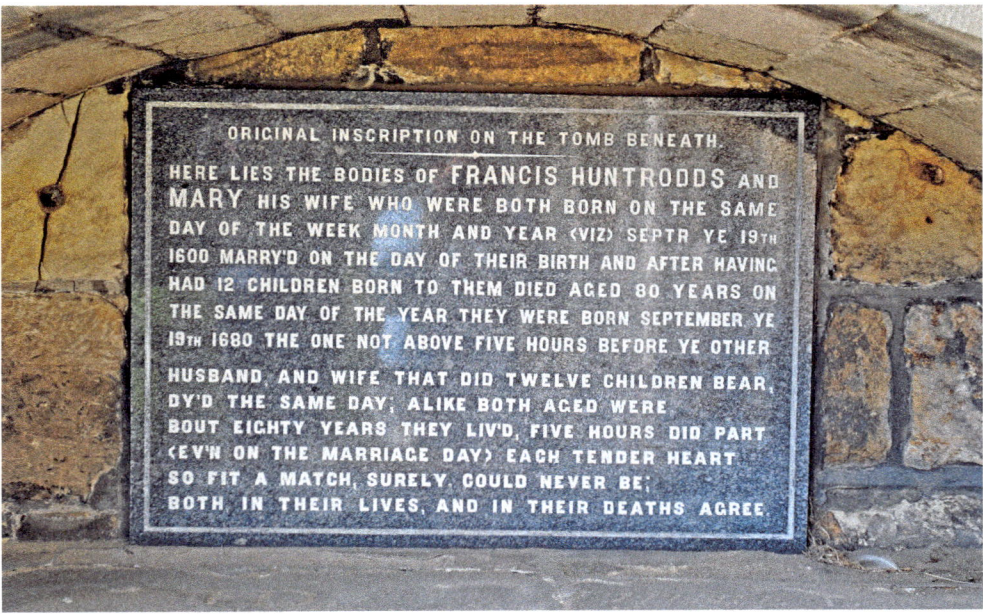

The mysterious grave of the Huntrodd family.

Whitby Abbey watches over a graveyard with many interesting tales.

contradictory inscription 'Here lies the body of Isaac Green whose body was lost at sea and never found.'

When writing *Dracula*, Bram Stoker would spend days wandering around chatting to locals about legends and curious tales which he then weaved into the fabric of his story. He was so inspired by the town that he couldn't help but add to the mystery of his tale by adding a little bit of Whitby lore. In the novel, the heroines (Mina and Lucy) are talking with their old friend, Mr Swales, when he makes mention of these 'empty' graves,

> Look here all around you in what airt you will. All them steans, holdin' up their heads as well as they can out of their pride, is acant, simply tumblin' down with the weight o' the lies wrote on them, 'Here lies the body' or 'Sacred to the memory' wrote on all of them, an' yet in nigh half of them bean't no bodies at all...

The churchyard also contains two sinister looking graves which are thought to contain the remains of pirates. These can be found close to the exit of the graveyard and are easily identifiable by the carved skull and crossbones on the end of the stone marker. In spite of the romantic sounding name, these graves do not contain the bodies of swashbuckling brigands. The skull and crossbones is a common piece of early funerary art that symbolised man's mortality.

As you explore further, you will find a grave marking the resting place of a famous local man – William Scoresby Snr. William grew up on a small farm near Pickering and was an agricultural labourer before his adventures at sea.

The famous pirate's grave – sometimes thought to be the resting place of Count Dracula.

The Scoresby Memorial.

In 1785 he joined the crew of the whaling ship named Henrietta and became captain in 1791. In 1806 he broke the British record for sailing furthest north, reaching latitude 80° 30', with his son William junior as chief mate.

A year later in 1807, he invented the barrel crow's nest to provide shelter for the navigator at the top of the main mast. This became an important feature in sailing and remained so until the invention of radar. The name was coined because the lookout platform resembled a crow's nest in a tree. William retired from whaling in 1823 after making his fortune and died six years later.

His son, William Scoresby Jnr, is also remembered on this gravestone although he died in Torquay and was laid to rest in Upton.

As you delve deeper among the weathered sandstone graves, there is another memorial that might catch your eye; nestled in a far corner of the churchyard is a grave made entirely of iron.

This is the grave of the engineer George Chapman and is one of only a few metal grave markers in the country. The grave at Whitby was commissioned before Chapman's death and cast at Baxtergate foundry. It has, sadly, fallen into some disrepair and no longer features the iron urn that once topped this impressive memorial.

St Mary's churchyard is now full and burials no longer take place here. It is a peaceful place containing many memories of days passed. No visit to Whitby would be complete without climbing the 199 steps and marvelling at the beautiful view of the sea and the town below.

3. Nautical Whitby

Life on the Sea

The modern tourist to Whitby would be surprised to hear the town described as a 'coal and whaling port', but that is what it was in the eighteenth and nineteenth centuries. Both of these industries were sea-based: the first was the great coastal trade of the east coast of England, the second involved a long and dangerous journey to Greenland and beyond. At one time Whitby was the sixth largest port in Britain.

There were other industries too, significant among them was the unpleasant one of making of oil (mainly from whales brought to Whitby from the North Atlantic). It is difficult to imagine now, but this industry was once located in and around Whitby's harbour. When it was at its peak, the smell from the boiling process was so great that people avoided it if they could. A commentator called the smell 'odious'. At this time it was only the locals who would have been put out by the smell, but many of whom found employment in one way or another from whaling.

The ships for the whaling industry were built in Whitby itself, but the town's shipbuilders constructed more colliers than they did vessels for whaling. There are references to ship building in Whitby as early as the seventeenth century, but it was the development of the coal trade in the succeeding century that gave shipbuilding the boost that it needed.

Colliers were ships built to carry coal and, again, in the eighteenth and nineteenth centuries, Whitby had a big share of this industry. The coal itself was not mined in Whitby but further north, particularly on the Tyne and the Wear at Newcastle and Sunderland. The coal owners needed the Whitby men for their skill at building and sailing ships; coal from the North East was delivered, in Whitby ships, to towns all along England's East Coast.

The first reference of Newcastle coal being transported in Whitby ships was as long ago as 1392. It was, of course, for the warming house and the abbot's lodging at Whitby Abbey!

One of the most famous ships ever built was constructed as a Whitby collier in around 1764 by the Whitby firm Thomas Fishburn. We know the ship today as the 'Endeavour', one of the two vessels used by Captain Cook on his three famous voyages of discovery.

By the time of the American War of Independence (1775–83) twenty ships a year were being built in Whitby. The trade was regarded as of such importance that the American, John Paul Jones, considered an attack on Whitby in an attempt to destroy the town's shipbuilding industry. This did not materialise but Jones did attack Whitehaven (on England's North-Western Coast) for much the same reason.

By the time of the Napoleonic Wars (1802–15) twenty-five ships per year were being constructed in Whitby; the peak year being 1802 when thirty-nine were under construction. As late as 1823, there were seven shipbuilding firms and they were supported by boat builders, sailcloth manufacturers and ropemakers. As the whaling industry declined and increasing amounts of coal were carried on the canals and the new railways, the demand for the kind of ships built in Whitby declined and the industry concentrated on Wearside and Tyneside.

Some of Whitby's colliers sailed across the North Sea, the Baltic, the Low Countries (Netherlands) and even to France and Germany.

However, the coastal coal trade was the main industry for Whitby ship owners. About 75 per cent of all coal produced in the North East was sent to London which, at the time, was growing into the largest city in Europe. William Cobbett, in his famous *Rural Rides* of 1821, described London as 'the great wen of all'. He was not being complementary. The 'wen' that Cobbett was referring to is a spreading cyst filled with sebaceous matter, generally located on the scalp! Clearly he did not think much of London, but the city needed coal and Whitby men were among the most important suppliers.

There's currently not very much to see in Whitby that recalls this once great industry, but if you go to London there are numerous reminders that Whitby men frequently visited with coal. The most well-known of these associations is a street, Seacoal Lane, which gave access to the 'Flete barges' into which the Whitby colliers disgorged their cargoes. The Flete River is now better known as the Fleet, which gives its name to Fleet Street, once synonymous with newspapers.

In addition to Seacoal Lane, there is an Old Seacoal Lane and close to this is Fleet Lane, the original site of the famous river. There is also a Newcastle Street quite close to the river, which recalls the town where much of the coal was mined and within walking distance of this there's a Whitby Street.

These street names bear scant witness to the importance of the landing of coal in this part of London, a commercial activity that goes back to at least 1228 when there is the first reference to a 'Secole Lane'. It is not known whether Whitby men were involved in the trade at that time but later they were frequent and welcome visitors to the capital. When London's supply of timber had been consumed, the city turned to coal and the easiest way to get reliable supplies was to bring it in by sea. London colliers joined in the trade too, as did places along the coast including Yarmouth; but Whitby, at one time, had almost 100 vessels plying the seas and loaded up with coal for London.

Of course, ships could not navigate the seas without billowing sails; another great Whitby seafaring industry was the making and repairing of sails. In effect, Whitby once had its own textile industry, which also included the making of ropes. This often surprises visitors from other parts of the country that have, in the past, excelled in these industries.

One such town is Warrington. It once made sailcloth from flax grown in what we now call Merseyside. Whitby imported some of its flax from the Baltic, also the source of commodities such as timber for shipbuilding, iron, pitch for sails and waterproofing, and hemp for ropes and canvas. All of these were either in short supply in England or not available here.

It makes sense that a shipbuilding and ship owning town should have its own connections with sailcloth makers. Unfortunately, although there has been some recent research, relatively little is known about how the industry operated in Whitby. However, it is known that at the time Whitby was building large numbers of colliers, flax was the best material out of which to make sails. The British alternative would have wool, but it absorbed water too well and would have blown itself out of shape with ease. It should be pointed out that parts of North Yorkshire were almost ideal for the growing of flax and it is known that Hutton Rudby specialised in the production of tough linen suitable for sailmaking. Was it there that the Whitby men obtained some of their sailcloth? Hutton Rudby was ideally placed to supply the seafaring trades of Teeside, Wearside and Tyneside, so why not the town at the mouth of the Esk?

It is not easy to separate the fibres of flax, which are later spun and woven into cloth from the tough, grassy plant from which they derive. A process known as retting was used.

Cotton might have been a contender for sailcloth, but it was not available in the eighteenth century when the Whitby shipbuilding industry was reaching its peak. In any case, in the early days, cotton cloths such as fustians were strengthened by the addition of linen warps.

Sailcloth made wholly from linen was tough, retained its shape in the wind, and could take pitch to make it even stronger. Sails were often black rather than white, not because they were dirty, but because they had been covered in pitch. Many Whitby vessels would have had black or grey sails, rather than the white ones of popular paintings.

The cloths produced in Whitby were often referred to as 'canvas' or 'canvass'. This was a strong course cloth of unbleached hemp or flax, particularly used for sails.

There must have been weavers' workshops in Whitby but where they might have been is not entirely clear. They may have been found in the little colonies of cottages that exist on both sides of the river. There are references to 'sail lofts' and 'sail yards' being located in the ship yards, which were located on the banks of the Esk.

Ship yards also made considerable use of rope that was made in Whitby from imported Baltic hemp. There is a street in Whitby called 'The Ropery', which reminds us of this old industry. Rope-works (or walks, as they were called) can be found in many towns and villages throughout England. Those in rural areas mostly produced rope for agriculture but Whitby's ropemakers made it largely for use at sea.

It was, of course, the whaling trade that was one of the industries to make Whitby a commercial centre. At one time, Whitby was the capital of the British whaling trade. Those who were employed in it (and the locally built ships themselves) were known as 'Greenland Whalers' because that is where they 'fished' for whales.

Getting to the Greenland and the Arctic was no mean feat when this industry operated. The ships were made of timber, yet had to travel thousands of miles through stormy seas to get to and from their hunting grounds.

The trade really began in the early 1750s. However, this first experiment with whaling was not a success; it came to a premature conclusion in 1762, but was revived five years later. The last whaler was decommissioned in 1837, the same year that Queen Victoria came to the throne. However, in those years, Whitby was transformed and the sum of man's knowledge of the sea, particularly the North Atlantic, was extended considerably because of Whitby men.

In his book, *A History of Whitby* (published in 1817, when whaling was still active and profitable), George Young commented, 'The success of the whale-fishery at its first commencement, and for many years after, bore no proportion to that of later years.'

A woodcut showing the 'flensing' of a whale, a process of removing its blubber before it is turned into oil.

He went on to mention that, at first, a ship was regarded as successful if it could bring home as few as four or five whales. An outstanding success was achieved by a Captain Banks who, in ten years, brought home sixty-five whales.

By the end of the eighteenth century, the number of whales taken to Whitby had increased tremendously. Young gives two examples. The first is for the ship known as the *Resolution*. It was owned and operated by the Scoresbys and in ten years (1803–13) it brought home 249 whales, which produced 2,034 tons of oil. The second example was the *Henrietta*, owned by the Kearleys. Between approximately 1807 and 1817 it brought back 213 whales, which produced 1,561 tons of oil.

In 1811 alone the *Henriette* brought back thirty-six whales – the greatest number by any Whitby ship in a single year. 1814 was the most successful single year for the industry as a whole: 172 whales were caught, brought to Whitby and processed to make 1,400 tons of oil, some of which was used in Whitby's early street-lighting system.

Despite these tremendous figures, the industry could not last. By 1834, only two whaler ships were left. Three years later and they were all gone, never to return to Whitby. However, the Greenland Whalers had transformed the town. They had contributed to the development of other industries, particularly shipbuilding, ancillary trades and banking. Similarly, the look of the town changed: the successful whalers (both owners and captains) built houses for themselves away from the old town, thereby creating the new Whitby, which so beautifully complements the old.

The whaling trade also did a great deal of damage to the ecology of the North Sea. This was not appreciated at the time, but the activities of the whalers of Whitby (and places

Whitby's famous whalebone arch, made of the jaw bones of a whale in commemoration of the town's most famous industry.

like it, especially in Northern Europe, and later the New World) were eventually seen to be unsustainable. Today, when we refer to a 'Whitby whale', it is not to a whale at all, but to a large portion of the more sustainable cod (as in cod and chips), or is it?

The first reference to Whitby as a centre of commerce can be traced to the early fourteenth century, when Italian merchants brought wine to trade with the monks at Whitby Abbey. But, the commodity that, at this time, was Whitby's biggest export might be a surprise – it was salt herring. We all know what has happened to the herring that used to occupy the western parts of the North Sea in vast numbers. They were fished, not quite to oblivion, but at one time that looked as if that might happen.

Then, at the beginning of the seventeenth century, Whitby acquired another industry, the mining of alum (something that, if current newspaper reports are to be believed, is about to be revived). Alum is a white crystalline chemical that has many uses, notably in the wool trade where it was used in the making of dyes.

Prior to the seventeenth century, alum was obtained from Italy and the Middle East. In the late Tudor period, the English realised that if they could find reliable source of alum, the rapidly expanding wool industry would benefit considerably and with it, the income of the national exchequer. A breakthrough was made at the beginning of the seventeenth century when aluminium sulphate, the most important ingredient of alum, was found in the Whitby area.

The first successful alum works was established north of Whitby at Guisborough but others soon followed. By 1823, there were six mines that produced 3,200 tons of alum. They employed around 600 workers in the industry which, to a considerable extent, paved the way for other industries in the North East of England (the chemical industries of Middlesbrough are the main beneficiary of this). However, improvements in the industry led to the demise of alum mining and processing. The last alum mine closed at Sandsend in 1871.

Someone once wrote that 'the only road to Whitby is the sea' and another observer commented that the market square isn't the centre of the town, it is the harbour. Everything revolves around the harbour; a large natural harbour protected from the winds of the North Sea by the great East and West Piers, which are dominated by their lighthouses.

It was around this harbour that all of the town's industries developed: fishing, shipbuilding, the carrying of coal, whaling, and so on. The harbour dominates Whitby, probably more than its great Abbey. The harbour is Whitby.

Did you know?
The original whale jawbone arch was erected after 1853 and is now in the Whitby Archives & Heritage Centre. The whalebone arch you see today was donated by the people of Alaska in April 2003.

Death Under the Sea

There are over 530 shipwrecks off the coast of Whitby. These wrecks have accumulated over the course of hundreds of years and have been brought about by a number of factors, including poor navigation, terrible weather, and two world wars. For a scuba diver, it is possible to visit the last resting place of a number of these vessels and, sadly, of their crew. During the First World War, the North Sea was to merchant shipping what the North Atlantic was during the Second World War. After the initial German advance in the First World War, France lost its own coalfields, which meant that the fuel needed to be obtained from elsewhere. The coalfields of the North East of England were mined and further aid and supplies were sent south along the coast to provide assistance for the French.

In an attempt to strangle this aid, the Imperial German Navy began laying mines off the East coast of England with the aim of sinking the merchant vessels that were providing aid. It was to prove to be a devastating blow to the British and the protection of this vital supply route had to be ensured.

During the December 1914 bombardment by the German battle cruisers *Derfflinger* and *Von der Tann*, they were accompanied by a smaller vessel, the *Kolberg*, which was busy laying a minefield that would claim between fifteen and twenty ships (both merchant vessels and Royal Navy minesweepers). The *Kolberg* was responsible for far more loss of life than what occurred during the onshore bombardment by its two companions.

The German Navy had laid immense minefields throughout the North Sea and the Admiralty knew that it would be an impossible task to clear them entirely. Instead, they would adopt a strategy of clearing a channel through the minefields that became known as the 'War Channel'. Initially it was a success, then the German fleet countered this strategy by developing a much more deadly and ferocious tactic. They sent out their U-boats!

Above: The *Kolberg*.

Left: Admiral Holtzendorff (1853–1919).

In the early part of the First World War, the U-boats sank approximately two ships a day. This led merchant ships to develop defensive methods to combat the threat posed to them and they soon armed themselves and had upon sighting a U-boat, their orders were to either run from it, or ram it! The submarine threat led to further advances in wartime technology and in 1916 the depth charge was developed, which resulted in the destruction of three U-boats.

In an attempt to turn the tide of war in the favour of the Germans, Admiral von Holtzendorff called for, and was granted, unrestricted submarine warfare in January 1918. He planned to sink 600,000 tons of shipping a month in an audacious plan to break the British supply routes and force them to surrender within six months. Within the first three months of this new offensive, 25 per cent of British shipping lay on the seabed.

Yet another new weapon was brought into play against the U-boats by the British and their allies. They would use planes to spot them, hunt them down and destroy them with ships loaded with depth charges.

On 28 August 1918, Oberluetnant Karl Dobberstein rested his U-boat, the UC-70, on the seabed a few miles from the harbour mouth at Whitby and waited silently. Dobberstein was a few weeks away from his thirtieth birthday and was already in command of his third U-boat. He was a successful commander, having been awarded the Iron Cross Second Class, Iron Cross First Class, and the Friedrich-August Cross for his service in the German Navy. He had taken command of the UC-70 on 8 June 1918 and had sunk eight ships during his command of that vessel.

Earlier that day, he had attacked a cargo ship, *Giralda*, approximately five and a half miles North West of Whitby. Six of the *Giralda's* crew were killed in the attack and an attempt to save the ship by beaching her failed. She was eventually declared a loss and sank half a mile off Kettleness point.

This attack alerted the Royal Navy and fledgling RAF to the presence of a U-boat in the area and, as a counter-measure, a Blackburn Kangaroo reconnaissance plane was launched from No. 246 Squadron RAF at Seaton Carew near Hartlepool. Dobberstein could only lie

A rare picture of a UC Type II coastal mine-laying submarine.

low and wait for his chance to slip away undetected, but this was not going to be a simple game of hide and seek. Not only had he sunk a nearby ship, but his submarine had also been damaged by a British mine and repairs were underway. Knowing that the odds were not stacked in his favour, Dobberstein and his crew waited in a tense silence.

Lieutenant E. F. Waring was piloting the *Blackburn* that day and, at 3 p.m., as he flew over Runswick Bay he spotted an oil slick on the surface and, at the head of the slick, he could see something under the water.

The bay is about twenty-seven metres deep and, lying submerged on the sandy bottom, was the unmistakable shape of a U-boat. Surely, this was the sub that had hit the *Giralda*! He flew overhead and released a 520 pound bomb on top of the UC-70. He had hoped for a direct hit, but unfortunately he had missed. The explosion was close enough to disable the already damaged submarine and Waring was able to guide the HMS *Ouse* onto its position, now marked by boiling air bubbles and oil leaking from the crippled U-boat.

The *Ouse* steamed at full speed into Runswick Bay and destroyed the UC-70 with its depth charges. None of the thirty-one men on board the submarine survived.

Many years later, one of the authors plunged into Runswick Bay with two air tanks strapped to their back and descended through the murky green water to the seabed. The light from the surface struggled to reach that far down and they had to use a torch to see.

A shoal of pollack swam past, their silver skins flashing in the torchlight, and then, rising out from the seabed, the dark hulk of the UC-70! Time had taken its toll on the stricken submarine, the conning tower had slipped from the hull and lay in the sand. The author finned along its length and then up onto the deck.

In the seventy odd years that it had laid there, in spite of the proliferation of sea anemones that had made the sub their home, the vessel was unmistakeable. Swimming forward along the hull, the author stopped at the unmistakable shape of the 88mm deck gun. It was frozen in position, never to fire again. They examined the breech and was surprised to see that, underneath the grime of oxidised metal, the alloy still shone brightly in the light of their torch.

In front of the gun, the author noticed a hatch that was folded open. The inner locking wheel was clear to see and they wondered in what circumstances this hatch had been opened. Had it been a desperate attempt by the crew to escape the wounded sub, or had it been opened by the Royal Navy divers led by Petty Officer Dusty Miller a fortnight after the sinking?

Peering into the hatch, sobered by the realisation that this was the last resting place of thirty-one men who had lived and died in a metal tube three metres wide and forty-nine metres long, the author could see nothing, only blackness. They continued along the hull and below them, set into the deck, were the mine laying tubes of the UC-70. Six tubes, responsible for laying the explosives that would cause so much danger along the War Channel.

Reflecting on the dive, what is saddening is that a great deal of the damage to the vessel has occurred, not through the depth charges of the HMS *Ouse*, but by salvagers who plundered the submarine for its scrap value, indifferent to the thirty-one deceased who still remain trapped inside the pressure hull of the UC-70.

The Three-Day Rescue

In times of war, British passenger ships are often pressed into military service; this chapter looks at one of those ships that will forever be a part of Whitby's history.

In 1906, the British India Steam Navigation Company became the proud owners of the newly completed SS *Rohilla*. It was named after the Pashtun Highlanders, the Rohillas. The vessel was 460 foot long and had been built in Belfast by the Harland and Wolff shipyard. It was intended to run the London to Calcutta service and its quadruple expansion steam engines (producing 8,000 indicated horsepower) would let the *Rohilla* reach top speeds of 16.6 knots.

The Rohilla was also designed to double up as a troopship in times of conflict and, in 1908, the ship was dubbed 'Troopship No. 6' and fitted with a radio receiver. In fact, it was one of the first ships owned by the British Indian Steam Navigation Company to have radio.

When war broke out across Europe in 1914, the *Rohilla* was quickly called into action and refitted as a hospital ship, with two operating theatres and X-ray facilities. It was now known as His Majesty's Hospital Ship *Rohilla*. But it was to have just a short life in that role.

On 30 October 1914, HMHS *Rohilla* set sail from Scotland towards Dunkerque, where it was to evacuate wounded soldiers from the front line. The weather that day was fearsome and strong gales vexed the journey. The North Sea during the First World War was, as we have seen, a dangerous place with many minefields having been laid; the *Rohilla* crept cautiously through the rough, rolling waves, with the wind howling around the decks.

The journey was especially taxing for the ship's captain, David Neilson, who had not navigated the North Sea before. He had to use dead reckoning on his journey due to the wartime conditions. Navigation lights were not permitted and the rough sea was throwing the ship about like a toy boat.

The last fix was taken as the *Rohilla* passed the Farne Islands; it steamed into the North Sea as the weather turned increasingly worse.

Rohilla was a passenger steamer of the British India Steam Navigation Company. After becoming a hospital ship she ran aground in October 1914.

The Whitby Coastguard, in his hilltop station close to the abbey, struggled to keep watch that night. Normally he would have had a fantastic view from the station across a vast expanse of sea, but in the dark and stormy night, at around 3:30 a.m., he could barely see a thing. He diligently kept his watch and then, in the darkness, he became aware of a murky shape on the sea. Darker than the surrounding water, he strained his eyes hard to make out this shape and recognised it as the silhouette of a ship; a ship running without lights, and running dangerously close to the treacherous reef known as Whitby Rock!

Before the war, Whitby Rock was marked by a bell buoy, but conflict had dictated that the bell be silenced and the light extinguished. The coastguard frantically tried to signal to the *Rohilla* to warn her of the impending danger, but there was no response so they could only look on in horror.

At 4.10 a.m. Captain Neilson was shaken by a tremendous impact against his ship; a deafening crash convinced him that he had struck a mine. With the safety of his 229 passengers at the front of his mind, he turned to the shore. Neilson had believed he was several miles from the coast, but the brutal weather and fierce waves had pushed the *Rohilla* closer and closer to the coastline throughout the night. Instead, the ship was about 600 metres from the shore when she hit the reef at full speed.

The coastguard desperately fired maroons into the air to alert the town of Whitby of the disaster that had just occurred. Time was of the essence, and it required as many people as possible to assist with the rescue.

On board the *Rohilla*, panic ensued. The impact of the ship striking the reef had broken its back in two places. Ice cold water rushed into the ship and chaos reigned. In one part of the ship, the onrushing water swept bunks and furniture into a group of men from the Barnoldswick branch of the St John's ambulance. Fifteen of these men had volunteered to join the *Rohilla* on its mercy mission but now, pinned down by the weight of the debris, twelve of these poor men lost their lives.

The survivors had rushed to the decks of the ship, rather than risk drowning in their cabins. Dressed only in what they stood up in and, in a few lucky cases, clutching a life jacket, they made their way to the decks. It was no better for them there.

By now the town of Whitby had been alerted to the ongoing tragedy and the No. 1 lifeboat, the *Robert and Mary Ellis* was being readied.

The *Robert and Mary Ellis* was a rowing lifeboat. Motor lifeboats were still in their infancy and the nearest of that kind was nearly fifty miles away at Tynemouth. New-fangled motor lifeboats weren't trusted at that time as the crews feared that they would be rendered useless by engine failure or propeller damage.

The coxswain of the *Robert and Mary Ellis* was Thomas Langlands and he realised that the sea conditions and weather were too bad to launch the lifeboat at that time. He had to explain this to his crew and inform them that they would wait until the morning to see if the conditions improved. It must have been a difficult decision for him to make, knowing that just over a mile away was a stricken vessel that needed his help.

On board the *Rohilla*, most of the survivors were clutching to the railings, or huddled in the ship's bridge trying to keep themselves safe from the sea. Great waves broke against the ship and enveloped it. For the hundreds of people lining the cliffs it was a terrible sight. They waited desperately for the lifeboat to arrive.

When dawn approached the sea was still too rough to launch the *Richard and Mary Ellis*, so Thomas Langlands made a brave decision. They would use the No. 2 lifeboat, the *John Fielden* instead. But instead of rowing out via the harbour mouth, they would go across the rough beach to Saltwick Nab, dragging the lifeboat.

Whitby harbour is protected by two long piers that are about ten metres high. The eastern pier is designed to protect the harbour from high seas, such as those being experienced when this tragedy occurred. At the shore end of the pier is a concrete breakwater which stops the sea from encroaching into the harbour at high tide. At low tide it is merely a wall between Tate Hill sands and the rough beach that leads to Saltwick Nab.

This was the biggest obstacle that stood in the way of the *John Fielden*; through extreme human effort, just after dawn when the tide was at its lowest, the lifeboat was dragged over the breakwater. The passage left its mark on the boat and it was damaged in two places, but the crew were undeterred. They were on their way to the site of the *Rohilla* and, at last, were able to launch and affect a rescue.

Meanwhile, on the *Rohilla*, the rough seas had destroyed all but one of the ship's lifeboats. An attempt at self-rescue was commenced and the last remaining lifeboat was launched.

Against all the odds, the crew of that small lifeboat made it to the shore, but the line that they had carried from the *Rohilla* had snapped. The situation had still not improved for the poor survivors, who were numbed by the cold and constantly battered by the immense seas.

Langlands and his team reached Saltwick Nab and set about launching the *John Fielden*. By now, the tide was coming back in and the currents were against them, but the brave crew struck out and were able to draw alongside the *Rohilla*. On that trip they succeeded in taking off seventeen souls and returning them to the shore.

By now the *Rohilla* was in a bad way: her back had been broken in two places and her stern had now become detached from the rest of the ship. Clutching desperately to it were about forty men who had been unable to reach the bridge for refuge. They were clad

A lifeboat (possibly the *John Fielden*) attempting to rescue passengers aboard the *Rohilla*.

in either pyjamas or whatever items they were able to scramble into when the ship had struck the reef. They were fighting against time and the tide.

The *John Fielden* had successfully brought seventeen survivors to shore but they had been carried, by the sea, half a mile northwards. The lifeboat was dragged back to Saltwick Nab and readied for its second rescue attempt. It struck out, and this attempt was to be even harder than the first.

The tide was rushing in and the crew, already massively fatigued, were battling the sea with every last reserve. They managed to draw alongside the *Rohilla* again and this time took off eighteen survivors. The *John Fielden* set off for shore, but was dragged northwards by the current again. When it beached, the lifeboat was severely damaged and the waves were approaching the foot of the cliffs. Langlands made the decision to abandon the *John Fielden* on the beach. The lifeboat was left to be pounded on the rocks, a sad end for such a heroic vessel.

The survivors, who had been clinging to the wreckage of the stern, were now being pulverised by the fierce waves. By now they were growing weak and the watchers on the cliff top could only watch in horror as, every so often, one of them would lose their grip on the railings and fall into the sea. Then, just before midday, a freak wave struck the stern with such a force that the spray and foam hid it from sight. It seemed never-ending, as it rushed over the stern and when the spray finally cleared there was no sign of the last of the survivors who had valiantly held onto the stern, patiently awaiting rescue. There was also no sign of the stern: it had been sent to the seabed by the awesome power of that giant wave.

The valiant lifeboat men were determined not to give up with their rescue attempts and they sent for another of Whitby's lifeboats. Led by Captain John Milburn, the Upgang lifeboat station relinquished its lifeboat and it was placed on its carriage and taken by road to the top of the cliffs. From here, it was lowered down the 200 foot cliffs to the beach where it would be able to launch. It was an amazing feat of human endurance; some who lowered the lifeboat suffered such terrible rope burns to their hands that their skin hung off.

Other lifeboats from Scarborough and Teeside had also been brought in to assist with the rescue. The Scarborough lifeboat arrived at 6.00 p.m. but, after eighteen hours at sea trying to get to the site, the crew were exhausted and unable to offer any assistance. They were forced to return home being towed by a steam trawler.

The Teeside lifeboat fared no better. She was a motor lifeboat but had been damaged by the rough seas and had to return home too, never having reached the *Rohilla*. By now it was dark and all that the rescuers could do was to wait and hope to get alongside what remained of the ship the next day.

When morning arrived, Thomas Langlands decided to take out the *Robert and Mary Ellis* again, but with a different strategy. They put out to sea and awaited the arrival of the steam trawler *Mayfly* from Hartlepool.

On board the *Mayfly* was the second coxswain of the Hartlepool lifeboat to assist with coordinating the rescue effort and together they planned to tow the *Robert and Mary Ellis* to within half a mile of the *Rohilla* and then make the approach to rescue the survivors. This plan, however, was deemed unworkable and the lifeboat returned to harbour.

The Upgang lifeboat, which had been lowered down the cliff, had made a valiant attempt to reach the *Rohilla* but, after an hour of fruitless rowing, the drained crew had

Rockets being fired from the shore to the *Rohilla* to assist in the rescue attempt.

Lifeguards attempt to get a line to the *Rohilla*. The powerful waves striking the ship caused it to quickly break apart.

The British Hospital Ship "Rohilla," on Its Way from Leith to Dunkirk to Bring Wounded British and Belgian Soldiers from the Battleground of Northern France, was Wrecked at Whitby on the East Coast of England. The Photograph Shows Life Guards Trying to Get a Line to the Wreck

to return to shore. There was only one option left for the rescuers – they would need a motorised lifeboat.

A telegram was sent to Tynemouth, forty or so miles away, where the Henry Vernon was stationed. This was a motorised lifeboat which, since it was commissioned, had led to the resignation of several old hands who had deemed it dangerous and untested.

When the telegram was received, the lifeboat was launched and set off for Whitby. Any fears about the engine failing were unfounded and it ran like a dream. After nearly nine hours at sea the Henry Vernon reached the *Rohilla*; the stricken ship was now in a bad way. It had already lost the stern and now the fore part of the ship had been lost to the sea.

All that remained was the bridge and the mid-section of the ship, kept in place on the reef by the weight of its boilers and engines. The time was 1.00 a.m., the lifeboat signalled to the survivors that help was at hand and then, realising that the sea conditions were still too bad, made for Whitby harbour where it was stripped of any items that were not necessary.

The crew of the lifeboat received refreshments and had a couple of hours to rest before they put out to sea again. The *Henry Vernon* was now carrying a cargo of gallons and gallons of oil.

The town of Whitby watched as the lifeboat motored out of the harbour and headed for calmer waters around the *Rohilla*. It reached a point within a few hundred metres of the wreck and then, to the astonishment of the watching crowds, turned seawards instead of towards the wreck as would be expected. At this point the crew took their cargo of oil and dumped it all into the sea.

The weight of the oil succeeded in flattening the waves and the crew brought the *Henry Vernon* around 180 degrees and then, at full speed, it raced towards the ship. They pulled alongside and began to take on board survivors from the ship as quickly as they could. The oil was beginning to break up and the waves were becoming treacherous once again.

At the last minute the captain boarded the lifeboat. He was, in true seafaring tradition, the last man off the ship. A great cheer was heard from the cliff top and the *Henry Vernon*, at last, turned around and left the wrecked *Rohilla* to the sea.

Suddenly, a huge wave hit the lifeboat broadside, risking a total capsize. The townspeople watching held their breath for what felt like an age. And then, the valiant *Henry Vernon* appeared, upright and making hard for Whitby, having kept hold of all on board.

The rocky reefs around Whitby have claimed many ships through time.

The survivors were put ashore at Whitby, where the townsfolk rallied around to help. They provided hot food and drink, blankets, and gave whatever they could.

The *Henry Vernon* turned back to sea. The captain had succeeded in rescuing the last survivors from the *Rohilla,* but his mission wouldn't be accomplished until he had landed his crew safely home. Many hours later he brought the little lifeboat back to the Tyne where, having heard of the daring rescue, thousands of people welcomed the lifeboat home and carried the crew on their shoulders through the streets.

Today, the *Rohilla* still has an important place in the heart of Whitby. Following the rescue, the town replaced its rowing lifeboat with a motorised one. The wreck can still be visited today, at low tide. It is worth the moderate walk along the reef, but keep an eye on the tide which can come in extremely quickly.

Of the 229 people on board the *Rohilla,* eighty-four perished; the memorial can be visited in Whitby's town cemetery. The Whitby Lifeboat museum has a display that chronicles the events of that tremendous rescue attempt and is well worth a visit.

Did you know?
The ship's cat was also rescued from the *Rohilla* by the captain. He was awarded the bronze medal by the Royal Society for the Prevention of Cruelty to Animals for this act.

A Bite to Eat

Whenever you mention the name Whitby to someone you are likely to get, with a knowing nod, the following replies, 'Ahh, Dracula' or 'Ahh, fish and chips'. Being a fishing town, it only stands to reason that Whitby is going to be famous for fish and chips and some of the finest examples anywhere in the world can be found in Whitby.

It is with some amusement that the rest of the world considers this wonderful peasant food of cod in batter with fried potato sticks to be a national dish of our island but, when you think about it, why shouldn't it be celebrated in such a way? It has no pretentions; it is what it is. But what is fascinating is how many different ways something so simple can be enjoyed and how people visit Whitby and queue for hours just to enjoy this basic staple meal. If you think you know fish and chips, think again!

When North Sea trawl fishing took off as a viable means of catching fish it led to a massive increase in its consumption in this country. Historically, those who lived on the coast would have had a diet high in fish compared to those who lived inland, but improved transport links such as the railway (brought to Whitby by, among others, George Hudson) meant that what was landed at Whitby could be on the fishmongers slabs of all of the big cities within a matter of hours.

Fish and chips developed as a working-class food that was nutritious and cheap; in the mid-nineteenth century fish and chip shops were springing up in towns and cities everywhere. Today, there are so many of the shops in Britain that it is estimated they outnumber McDonald's restaurants by eight to one!

Whitby remains an important fishing port to this day.

The Quayside – a fish restaurant that was once the Whitby Public Lending Library.

Right: The Magpie Café.

Below: The famous Magpie Café – long queues outside are commonplace due to the restaurant's excellent reputation.

There are approximately fifteen fish and chip shops in Whitby and, in 2014, one of Whitby's own, the Quayside, won the twentwhy-sixth annual National Fish and Chip Awards to be named Britain's fish and chip shop of the year. That particular restaurant has an interesting place in the history books of Whitby as the building, which dates back to the 1820s, was once a public bath house, museum and library.

The library was visited by Bram Stoker, who found among the books on the first floor, the inspiration for his famous horror story *Dracula*.

Just a short stroll down the road from Quayside and you will probably find Yorkshire's most famous chippy – the Magpie Café. Before you reach it, you will have noticed a queue of people spilling down the stone stairs and backing up along the street as they all await their turn to be called forward and seated at a table in the restaurant that was proclaimed by Rick Stein as, 'The place that opened my eyes to how good a chip shop could be.'

The Magpie Café is situated in a tall black and white building with bay windows on its first floor. It overlooks the harbour and the fish market and has been a part of Whitby's seagoing community since it was built in 1750; it has acted as a Merchant's House, a pilotage (where pilots would wait for their instructions to guide ships into Whitby harbour), and has been a shipping office.

If you don't like to queue for your food there is a much quicker takeaway counter at street level, where you can get your Magpie fish and chips and take a stroll down the harbourside.

It would be impossible to talk about fish and Whitby without mentioning kippers. Love them or loathe them, Whitby is famous for kippers and there is often nothing better than a quick stroll up Henrietta Street (near to the 199 steps) and take in that wonderful aroma of oak smoke.

If you were to follow your nose it would lead you to the door of a tiny smokehouse nestled under the cliffs. This is Whitby's only traditional smokehouse, established in 1872 by William Fortune. The smokehouse remains in the Fortune family to this day.

The kipper is a smoked herring which, when it arrives at the smokehouse, is split down the middle, gutted, soaked in brine, and then threaded onto sticks where it hangs in the smokehouse for about eighteen hours before it is ready to be sold.

I was fortunate enough to be allowed to peer inside the smokehouse where racks of kippers hung from the ceiling. The inside of the small room was covered with sticky black tar from the smoking process and the smell was enough to make me hungry.

Fortune's kippers have a huge celebrity following from famous chefs (such as Rick Stein, James Martin, and the Two Fat Ladies) to the royal family, and who can blame them? There really is nothing better than traditionally smoked kippers for breakfast when visiting Whitby.

Fish have always been big business in Whitby, but if heading out to the icy North Sea on a trawler isn't really your thing, you could always have a go at catching your own.

Since their construction in 1913, the wooden pier extensions have offered local anglers the opportunity to catch a wide range of fish that has included bass, pollock, and mackerel. But, when the winter fishing season arrives the best catches are to be had because the cod move in. It is said that the biggest cod go to those who are brave enough to stand on the pier on the coldest of days.

Right: Fortunes – Whitby's only traditional smokehouse, which has been working for over 139 years.

Below: Whitby kippers in the smokehouse.

Anglers trying their luck from the East Pier.

Crab fishing (picture courtesy of Ben Abbatt).

Even so, in the summer months, if you were to walk along the harbourside you would find hundreds of holidaymakers getting involved in the delights of fishing, dropping their crab lines alongside the weathered posts and patiently waiting for a curious crab to investigate the bag of bait before it is hoisted out of the water and plopped into a waiting bucket.

Most of the time these crabs are tiddlers and are soon released, but every once in a while you will hear gasps of excitement and a resounding cheer as someone lands a monster crab of such size that it can only be destined for the dinner table!

The World's Oldest Pier

While exploring the old part of Whitby you may find yourself strolling down a narrow alleyway that leads to Tate Hill Sands. At the end of the narrow gap a modest stone pier stretches out in front of you, decorated by a large wooden anchor at the far end. This is Tate Hill Pier and could be, some have claimed, the oldest pier in the world.

Previously known as Burgess Pier after the burgesses of Whitby (residents of the town with full rights of citizenship), Tate Hill Pier is believed to have been built in the 1190s when it was nothing more than a jumble of stones with a wooden framework. However, in spite of its crude appearance it still served a useful function for the early fishing vessels of Whitby who were able to land their catch and protect early vessels from the sea.

The timber anchor situated on Tate Hill Pier was caught in the nets of a Whitby trawler close to Robin Hood's Bay.

Tate Hill Pier is a popular vantage point to watch the various ships and boats of Whitby pass by.

Whitby harbour.

The pier continued to serve a vital role in the fishing industry and, in 1301, a pier master was employed who was able to regulate the use of the pier, indicating it was in significant use.

The pier underwent a series of modifications through time. It was rebuilt in stone in 1632 before being extended to a length of 105 yards in 1766; today, the join can still be seen where the extension was made.

When Whitby's East and West piers were built, Tate Hill Pier's significance began to diminish. Between 1822 and 1863 the pier was the mooring point of the lifeboat, before moving to a purpose-built lifeboat station.

The pier later became a tourist location: a place where people could stroll and take in the view of Tate Hill Sands where, in August 1855, a Russian schooner called the Dimitry ran aground. Photographs were taken of the stricken vessel from the pier by the famous Whitby photographer, Frank Meadow Sutcliffe. These photos were seen in 1890 by Bram Stoker who, being inspired by the wreck, renamed it the Demeter.

Today's visitors to Tate Hill Pier can enjoy watching the flotilla of boats toing and froing in the harbour. During the Whitby Regatta it provides a good vantage point from where the various races and boats can be viewed. It is an unassuming location now, but without it, maybe Whitby wouldn't have become the town it is today.

4. Notable People of Whitby

Religious Folk

St Hilda

Whitby has been the home of a perhaps surprisingly large number of well-known people but none of them can surpass St Hilda, the first abbess of Whitby. The great abbey buildings, which dominate the town, have little to do with St Hilda as she lived many years before this monastery was founded.

The present Whitby Abbey was a Norman foundation, though it was not granted abbey status immediately. It was home to Benedictine monks and in this second incarnation, it was to become one of the great religious houses of England.

The religious house founded by St Hilda dates from the seventh century, AD 657 to be precise. It was a double house, one in which both men and women worshipped together but who, otherwise, lived apart. This was a way of monastic living that was revived by the English monk, St Gilbert of Sempringham in the twelfth century.

The Whitby of St Hilda's time was a very different place to the town we know today. You may remember the place name was different, it was known as Streonaeshalch. The name Whitby did not evolve until the Normans arrived and means 'the white settlement'.

St Hilda was the second daughter of Prince Hereric (the nephew of King Edwin of Deira, and later king of Northumbria). Edwin later became the 'bretwalda' (the 'Britain-wielder', or overlord of all the kings) of the island south of Hadrian's Wall. St Bede, who was almost a contemporary of St Hilda, tells us that she was born in around 614 at a time of great unrest in what became the North East of England. It may be that, because of this, Hilda was not born in her own country and when she was a young woman she may have had to spend some more time away from the North East.

Only two years after the birth of Hilda, her great uncle, the king, defeated the rival king of the neighbouring kingdom of Bernicia and united the two kingdoms into Northumbria. As her father had been killed (poisoned at the court of Elmet, a small kingdom in what is now Yorkshire), Hilda was brought up at the court of King Edwin. He remained on the throne until 633 when he, in turn, was killed in battle by the pagan king of Mercia, at Heathfield, near Doncaster.

However, Hilda was living in interesting times in terms of what was happening to religion. Although the Romans had introduced Christianity into Britain, much of the country had fallen back into paganism because of the success of the Anglo-Saxon invasions. Christians in Ireland had not been influenced as much by the pagan invaders and they had sent missionaries to England, a number of whom were active in the North and over the border in what became Scotland.

In fact, under the influence of the queen, and St Paulinus (who had been sent to the North on missionary work) King Edwin had converted to Christianity at York, his capital, in 627. Bede tells us that a temporary wooded church was built on the site of the great Minster in York and it was there that Edwin was received into the church by St Paulinus, who is known to us as 'the apostle of the North'.

When Edwin fell from power St Paulinus fled from the North East, taking the queen and Hilda (then a nineteen-year-old girl) with him to Kent, which had remained Christian. It is thought that Hilda continued with her Christian education, which had been started at Edwin's court; by the time we come across her again, Hilda was a nun with a growing reputation for her piety and good sense. Aidan of Lindisfarne, sent her an invitation to travel North to help in the foundation of a new monastic institution on the banks of the river Wear, in what is now County Durham.

Unfortunately we do not know where this abbey was, but it was here that Hilda learned the traditions of the Celtic Church, the Christian tradition of her own country. Hilda was then appointed abbess of Hartlepool, another Celtic monastery of which we know little, though the ancient graveyard of this place has been discovered and studied.

After making a success of the venture at Hartlepool, Hilda was chosen, in around 657, to be the founding abbess of Whitby. This was in the time of Finan, Aidan's successor at Lindisfarne. The site of Hilda's abbey is not known for certain but recent archaeological work suggests that it occupied the same site as the present abbey. As a Celtic foundation, it would have been run on very different lines to the Benedictine rule that applied in the later building. Hilda enjoyed great success and a number of the men who joined her community rose to high office in the early Church. These included John of Beverley, the bishop of Hexham, and Wilfrid, the great bishop of York, both of whom were canonised.

While managing the community at Whitby, Hilda's fame spread. She was consulted by kings and princes and became famous for her wisdom. In addition, she had a great concern for ordinary folk, as the story of Caedmon will show. Bede wrote that, 'All who knew her called her 'mother', because of her outstanding devotion and grace.'

Of course, Hilda's life, as is the case with the poetic Celts, became the stuff of myth and legend. There are many stories that are told of her and they reveal the great regard that the people of Whitby had for her. One of these stories involves a comment that when the birds fly over the abbey, they dip their wings to St Hilda.

Another story involves Hilda dealing with a plague of snakes. Saints and snakes seem to go together. The stories that revolve around them are closely related to the themes of good and evil found in medieval miracle plays. I do not need to tell you that St Hilda represents 'good' and that the snakes, with their devilish associations, represent 'evil'.

Most of us know about the story of St Patrick who banished snakes from Ireland. The story of St Hilda, and her snakes, is less well known but, when you visit Whitby, you can't escape from snakes. You will find them on the coat of arms of Whitby council and you will have seen them (inanimate and petrified, thank goodness) in some of the tourist shops in the centre of town.

According to the legend, St Hilda, much to the relief of people who lived there, turned a plague of snakes into stone. However, Whitby is famous for its fossils. It is on Yorkshire's Jurassic coast and the number of ammonites that that have been found there must be beyond calculation. A number of the best examples, often washed up on the beach, have been worked by locals. They have fashioned 'heads' onto these stone ammonites and the finished snakes have been palmed off as the stone snakes attributable to St Hilda. In fact, one of the fossil ammonites is known as 'Ammonite Hildoceras' – St Hilda's ammonite.

When we think of St Hilda and Whitby, we generally think of one thing, the Synod of Whitby. Oswy, a later king of Northumbria, chose Whitby for the Synod. It was the first great meeting of what was to become the English Church and the king made his choice of venue because of the reputation of Hilda.

According to Bede, the Synod took place in AD 663/4. However, it has been worked out that this gathering of churchmen, who came from all over our islands, actually met at either the end of September 663, or early October of the same year. The Synod was one of the most important Christian meetings that has taken place in Britain. Its objective was to address the many differences which existed between the Celtic and the Roman Churches.

Little is known about the role of St Hilda at the Synod of Whitby, but she ruled wisely over her monastic house for about twenty-two years. In that time it became one of the most influential religious and educational centres in the country. She died in 680 at the age of sixty-six. Her saint's day is celebrated in mid-November.

Caedmon

To be associated with one the great saints of the English church might be enough for most places, but Whitby is also recognised as the home to Caedmon, who has been described as 'the first English poet' and 'the father of English song'. It was actually St Hilda who recognised the God-given gifts of a lay brother, a resident of her great abbey.

Little is known of the early life of Caedmon, but he wrote in the language of the Anglo-Saxons and, though little has survived of his work, Bede implies that Caedmon produced much divine poetry from the starting point of total illiteracy. His story starts in St Hilda's abbey, where he cared for the animals at the monastery. Of course, this was no zoo: the abbey needed milk, butter, cheese and eggs and Caedmon was charged, under Hilda's bailiff, to work in what in later monasteries would be regarded as the grange. It may be that the remains of the 'home farm' about a mile south of the abbey is the place where Caedmon worked.

According to Bede, Caedmon was illiterate and ignorant of 'the art of song'. On one occasion, Caedmon retired early to bed because he could not join in with his colleagues at the abbey, who were enjoying an evening singing. During the night someone appeared to Caedmon while he was asleep and asked him to sing a song about the creation.

At first Caedmon refused, saying that he knew nothing about song. By the time he had woken up, a song in praise of God and His creation, the very subject suggested to him in his sleep, was firmly fixed in his mind. He told the bailiff and then likely recited his poem. He may even has sung it, but the bailiff (an educated man) was astounded by what he heard and told Hilda about what had happened.

St Hilda had a reputation of being very caring towards those with whom she worked and whom she met. If a young brother in her care had written something about the creation, and God's role in it, she felt that she had to hear it. It might be that Caedmon's words were being inspired by God.

Caedmon was sent for and asked to recite his poem. It was not a simple poem and it used language that a man of his status would not normally use. St Hilda was surprised and delighted at the same time. We are told that she thought Caedmon's words were indeed divinely inspired, but she also decided to set Caedmon a task. She asked that he write another poem and gave him a biblical subject on which he was to produce something for the following day.

The next day Caedmon went to see the abbess and delivered his new poem. Hilda was now convinced that the poems were divinely inspired and she ordered that he take the vows necessary to become a monk. She also made arrangements for Caedmon to be taught sacred history and doctrine.

So far as we know, Caedmon used the stories he was told, and later those he read for himself, to produce more poems, but only part of one of his works survives. This is *Caedmon's Hymn*, the subject of the first of his dreams. There are many translations but this version, which is taken from a number of them, conveys the thoughts of the poet in an accessible way.

> Now the words of the Father of Glory must honour the guardian of heaven,
> the might of the architect, and the minds of his purpose,
> the work of the Father of Glory – as He is the
> beginning of wonders (and He)
> established, the eternal Lord,
> He first created for the children of the Earth
> Heaven as a roof, the holy creator
> Then the middle-earth, the guardian of mankind,
> the eternal Lord, afterwards appointed
> for men among the Lands, the Lord Almighty.
>
> *Caedmon's Hymn*

On first reading this, it could be thought that almost anyone could have produced verse of this kind, but it has to be remembered that these words are regarded as the first poetry that has survived to us in English. Given the levels of literacy at the time, it is not suprising they were produced in a religious house. These places were not only concerned with religion, abbeys like the one at Streonaeshalch were the centre of their community, interested in the well-being of the people who lived there, whatever their status.

Caedmon has not been forgotten. After his death, which took place between 679 and 684, the abbey church became a place of pilgrimage not only to St Hilda, but also to Caedmon. There is a beautiful statue in St Mary's churchyard that was erected in 1898 to his memory. Of course, a number of official bodies in Whitby are named in his honour, including the local school. How great it must be to attend a school named after the father of English poetry.

Lastly, although almost all of Caedmon's work is now lost, his divine poem is credited with helping to spread Christianity to all of the British Isles. His name was once very well-known and it should be coupled with 'Caedmon of Whitby'.

The Caedmon Cross in St Mary's churchyard. A relief of Caedmon is carved into the cross.

Explorers and Sea-Goers

It has been shown that Whitby's prosperity over the years has gone hand-in-hand with the sea. The town's long industrial and commercial history is not merely the story of its oldest industry (fishing and the processing of fish), as has remained the case in many other maritime centres. Both of these industries survive to this day, but Whitby men demonstrated degrees of ingenuity not confined to the industries that once existed in the town.

Whitby men have had an impact on the world far greater than might have been expected from a town that was cut off and insular from the rest of the country. The solitude of the Whitby of monastic times was not for them. As we have seen, the men of Whitby were sons of the sea. They looked to the world and it is to Whitby's proud place in the history of the world that we must turn now.

Captain Cook

It should be said at the outset of this story that Captain James Cook was not actually born in Whitby. However, he is one of those figures who transcends such things. People claim him, not only in the North East of England, but also in Australia, New Zealand, the Pacific and Canada.

James Cook was born in Marton-in-Cleveland (now part of Middlesbrough) in 1728. His father, also named James, was a Scottish farm labourer, who first moved to Marton and then went on to Great Ayton and to Airey Holme Farm. It was clear that James was an intelligent

The impressive statue of Captain James Cook looks over the harbour where he began his seafaring career.

boy and in 1736 his father's employer, a Mr Thomas Skottow, paid for him to attend the local school, where he excelled. In 1741 James accepted a position with his father who was, by then, Mr Skottow's farm manager. Four years later, he travelled to the fishing village of Staithes to be apprenticed as a shop boy to William Sanderson, a grocer and haberdasher.

Little is known of James's time there but he must have impressed Mr Sanderson because the shop keeper recommended the young man to John and Henry Walker who were Quaker ship owners engaged in Whitby's burgeoning coal trade. There is a story that James first saw the potential of the sea when looking out of the window of the shop in Staithes but, in truth, there were plenty of opportunities for young men in the coastal coal trade and it seemed that James was just the sort of person that the Walkers were looking for.

James began a three-year apprenticeship in the service of the Walker brothers. A merchant navy apprenticeship involved practical work as well as studies; so we find James at sea aboard one of the brother's colliers (his earliest known vessel being the Freelove, which sailed between the Tyne and London) and attending the school operated by the Walkers in the attic of their house on what is now Grape Lane in Whitby.

At the time Mrs Walker, the mother of the two brothers, was ill and the apprentices were not allowed in the house. They had to get into the attic (set out like a small classroom) from a rope ladder! Given what James was there for, this might have been part of the training, but, as an apprentice, James lived at the house so he might not have all that far to climb!

The house in Grape Lane is now the Captain Cook Memorial Museum and it is well worth a visit, not only for its Cook connections, but also for the recreations demonstrating how a

Captain Cook's old lodgings and former school, currently a museum dedicated to his life.

successful ship-owning family lived at this time. While James was at Grape Lane he applied himself, with the support of his employers, to algebra, geometry, trigonometry, navigation and astronomy, all skills he would need if he was to become a successful sea captain.

After his apprenticeship, James served the Walkers in the Baltic trade which, at this time, was very important to the British economy. Coal was exported from the North East of England but the Baltic was the source of timber, iron, pitch and a number of other commodities. The work was challenging but, in 1752, James passed his mates exams and was appointed to that position on the collier brig, *Friendship*.

Three years later, at the age of twenty-seven, he was offered command of his first ship. It was the passport to future prosperity but James had other ideas. He volunteered for the navy which he entered, as an ordinary seaman, at Wapping on 17 June 1755. It was not long before his talents were recognised and he became a master, achieving the rank of lieutenant in 1759. In fact, Cook was one of the first men in the navy to rise from the ranks to command a vessel.

At this time Britain was rearming for another war with France. It was to be known as the Seven Years War (1756–63) and, in a number of respects, it can be regarded as the first modern world war. It was fought in Europe, India, North America, Canada, the Caribbean, and South East Asia, and the British (with their European allies) from a less than inspiring start, ended up on top.

The French were defeated just about everywhere and 1759 has been called 'the most glorious (year) in the annals of our History', on account of the great victories gained by

British troops in various parts of the world. 'One is forced to ask every morning', said Horace Walpole, 'what victory there is for fear of missing one'.

In the same year, James Cook was playing his part in the proceedings in Canada. Continual small-scale warfare had been going on for some years between the French and British settlers. Most disputes were about boundaries. The British had the Thirteen Colonies – the foundation upon which the United States was built – which extended along the Atlantic coast of America to the Alleghany mountains in the west.

The French has established colonies in Canada and Louisiana. In 1749 they claimed all the lands west of the Alleghenies' driving out the British settlers. The French general, Montcalm, built a line of forts from Louisiana and Canada, but the British responded by sending out General Braddock who was defeated and killed, in 1756, at Fort Duquesne which was situated on the Ohio river. Two years later the British, assisted by Americans under George Washington, took the fort and renamed it Pittsburgh in honour of the first William Pitt (later Lord Chatham) and so it remains.

In 1759, Pitt appointed General Wolfe to command the English army in Canada. He was instructed to drive the French out of that country and James Cook was to play a part in the victory. Using his skill as a surveyor and cartographer he planned safe routes for British ships along the St Lawrence River. He was able to demonstrate that it was possible to take Quebec using the river under the cover of darkness. Cook was present at the capture of the fort and the city which were taken by a skilful manoeuvre, led by Wolfe, who was killed at the moment of victory. Five days later, with Montcalm also dead, Quebec surrendered after which Canada was lost to the French.

Cook's actions came to the notice of the Admiralty. They ordered him to undertake a full survey of the seas around Newfoundland, an exercise that was not improved on for almost 200 years. Then, in 1766, the Admiralty and the Royal Society turned to Cook for the three special voyages for which he is now famous. He was appointed commander of HM *Bark Endeavour* which had been built as a collier in his old stamping ground of Whitby.

At the time, although more trouble was brewing in North America, Britain was the undisputed naval power in the world. What Cook was charged to do was, in effect, to undertake the explorations which would enable Britain to establish another New World.

This name had been descriptive of the America's (a discovery had been made less than 300 years before). Now, Britain stood at the brink of another adventure, one in which she would be the leader, rather than the follower. England, for there was no Britain at this time, had not been in a position in the late fifteenth and early sixteenth centuries to participate in the European expansion into the New World. Things were rather different in the mid-eighteenth century.

Cook, in a series of three brilliant voyages, mapped lands and seas from Hawaii, in the Pacific, to New Zealand, in greater detail than had been achieved before. He also sailed far north in the Pacific in search of the western entrance to the North West passage, though in this he failed and lost his life.

The first of his adventures came in 1768–71 when he carried a Royal Society expedition to Tahiti to observe the transit of Venus across the Sun. This was publically known from the outset, but the Admiralty had, secretly, charged Cook with finding the 'Great Southern Continent' which, it was believed, existed at the 'bottom of the Globe'.

After completing the work associated with the transit, Cook circumnavigated and charted New Zealand, ascertaining that it was not part of a large landmass. It is thought that he came very close to sighting Antarctica but, later, he surveyed the East coast of Australia and claimed it for Britain. In addition, he surveyed the straight between Australia and New Guinea and the voyage was completed by way of Java and the Cape of Good Hope.

On this voyage, Cook was probably the first European to see the East coast of Australia. He landed at, and named, Botany Bay (the name deriving from the wealth of plant life there). It was at this time that the expedition almost came to grief. Cook had no knowledge of the Great Barrier Reef (off the East coast of Australia) and when he set sail for the Dutch port of Batavia on his way to New Guinea, his ship ran into the Reef and began taking in water. The ship was saved when cannon were thrown overboard and the large gash in the hull stuffed with old sailcloth. Cook managed to get the ship to Australia where the ship was repaired.

Cook was promoted to the rank of commander and, on his second voyage, he sailed round Antarctica (1772–75) and discovered several Pacific island groups, including the New Hebrides, New Caledonia and Tahiti. Thanks to his dietary precautions, which included measures against scurvy (a disease caused by a deficiency in Vitamin C), there was only one death among his crew. It is thought that Cook's insistence on taking on-board fresh vegetables and fruit whenever he could, would have helped prevent scurvy, but it is possible that his purchase of large amounts of sauerkraut may have had an effect. At first the men would not eat it, but when they saw the officers dining on sauerkraut they changed their minds.

The third voyage (1776–79) aimed to find a passage around the northern coast of North America from the Pacific. Attempts had been made to find the so-called North West Passage from the east but without success. It was thought that the passage might be found from the West; Cook was ordered to sail to the South Atlantic, round the Cape and into the Pacific where, in 1778, he became the first European to visit the Hawaiian Islands. Cook named them the Sandwich Islands after the Earl of Sandwich, one of his patrons.

Captain Cook and his crew were welcomed by the Hawaiians, who were not only fascinated by the European ships, and their use of iron, but it is likely that they regarded their visitors as gods. At this stage there was no sign of the trouble that lay ahead, but Cook wanted to continue with his expedition. His ships (there were two of them this time: HMS *Resolution* and *Discovery*) were reprovisioned in exchange for iron and they set off to the North.

Cook surveyed the West coast of North America from 45" North, as far as Icy Bay in the Baring Strait. However, he failed to find the North West Passage and was forced to return to Hawaii because of the oncoming winter and a threat of mutiny from his men. What was thought to be a safe harbour, at Kealakekua Bay, was located but neither Cook nor his crew realised that the Bay was the sacred harbour of Lono (the Hawaiian god of fertility) and that festivities in the god's honour were about to take place.

At first, Cook and his men were welcomed as they had been before, but within a month the Hawaiians had become disaffected by the Europeans, many of whom behaved very badly. Perhaps Captain Cook should have done something about this but, soon, a crewman died. With this, the mystique that surrounded the Europeans (their god-like status) had broken and relations between the parties became strained.

Little Park.

At the top of Pannet Park you will find the South Seas Garden with its carved Maori to celebrate Cook's discoveries in the Pacific.

In February 1779, the British ships sailed from the Bay but rough seas damaged the foremast of the Resolution which, after only a week, returned to Hawaii. The natives greeted Cook and his men with stones and, within a short space of time, a small cutter vessel was stolen from the Resolution and a difficult situation became a dangerous one.

Cook was determined to get the vessel back and he entered into negotiations with the emboldened king of the Hawaiians. A chief was shot to death by the British and a mob descended on Cook's party. The captain, and his men, fired at the Hawaiians but they were soon overwhelmed. A few managed to get back to the ship, but Cook was brutally killed. The British retaliated by bombarding the island and firing muskets at the natives. About thirty were killed.

This tragic incident brought an end to the life of one of the greatest explorers and seamen that have ever lived. Cook circumnavigated the world twice and he did more than any other navigator to add to the knowledge of the Pacific and the Southern Ocean. Cook vowed 'to sail as far as I think it possible for a man to go', words which demonstrate his determination to satisfactorily complete the tasks given to him by the Admiralty.

The name of Captain James Cook RN will be remembered for as long as we are interested in the story of the exploration of the world. He was, in his day, the equivalent of Neil Armstrong and Buzz Aldrin who, in July 1969, were the first two men to set foot on the moon.

Whitby can be proud of its adopted son, James, and his great achievements. He is certainly remembered in both Australia and New Zealand and also in Canada and the USA. The cottage, Airey Holme, had been the boyhood home of Captain Cook and was purchased in 1933, dismantled and taken to Melbourne, in Australia, where it can now be seen, fully restored, in Fitzroy Park in the city. The Americans has wanted to buy it but its last English owner refused to sell it to them. She allowed it to go to Australia because, as she said, 'it is still in the Empire', then Australia gained full independence from Britain in 1901. The erection of the cottage was the centrepiece of Melbourne's centenary celebrations, which took place in 1934.

There are places all over the world named after Captain James Cook, including the Cook Islands; the Cook Mountains in Antarctica; Cook's River in New South Wales, Cook's Bay in Canada; Mount Cook in the USA; and the Cook glacier, also in Antarctica. In addition, there are two towns in Australia named after Cook, one in New Zealand, one in Canada and one in the USA.

William Scoresby Snr and William Scoresby Jnr
No other man of Whitby has achieved such fame, but Captain Cook is not the only individual from the town who became known for his associations with the sea. The Scoresby family (father and son and both named William) has produced two men who should not be forgotten, not only in Whitby, but their contribution was such that they should not be forgotten elsewhere. They were inventors, scientists and explorers, as well as very successful whaling captains.

William Scoresby Snr (1760–1829) came from a relatively humble background, growing up in nearby Pickering. He was an agricultural labourer before going to sea. The latter was becoming a way out of poverty for ambitious youths and in 1785 William joined the crew of the whaler, Henrietta, becoming its master six years later. At this time Whitby was the pre-eminent centre of whaling in Britain and he enjoyed spectacular success as a captain and as an Arctic explorer.

1807 was a remarkable year for the senior William Scoresby, he achieved two outstanding successes. He took his ship, the Resolution (not the ship sailed by Captain Cook), with his son as chief mate, as far North as any ship have ever been before. The ship reached 80'30' and only 500 miles from the North Pole. It was at this time that he invented the crow's nest. The son, also named William, was born in 1789 at Cropton, near Whitby, and took his first sea trip with his father at the age of eleven,who, by this time, was becoming a successful man. In 1806, at the age of seventeen, he joined his father on the Resolution as first mate, sharing with him his successes of the following year.

William Jnr was a studious boy and, in between work for his father, he studied meteorology and the natural history of the polar regions. He attended lectures in 1806–07 at the University of Edinburgh, putting this knowledge into practice when he was at sea. After publishing a number of papers, and while still a very young man, he was elected to the Wernerian Natural History Society, an elite offshoot of the Royal Society of Edinburgh.

He got married in 1811 at the age of twenty-two and at the same time he succeeded his father as the master of the Resolution. It was then that he made his well-known observations on snow and crystals. In 1813 he established that the Polar Ocean has a warmer temperature at depth when compared to that at the surface. He started corresponding with the scientist Sir Joseph Banks but continued visiting the Arctic regions, especially Greenland, where in the early 1820s he produced the first reliable charts for the East coast of the island.

Before this, like his father before him, he made, an improvement that considerably affected the lives and safety of all of those who were employed on the sea. His improvement was to the compass (a vitally important instrument for sailors) and in succeeding years, he continued this work and the related subject of terrestrial magnetism. He wrote a number of books on whaling and the polar regions, a great number of articles of a scientific nature, and was elected a Fellow of the Royal Society.

However, in 1822 his wife died and Scoresby joined the Church, and attended the University of Cambridge where he received his degree in 1825. There can't have been many people who had been elected FRS before they were awarded their degree! William continued his scientific studies throughout his life but he became interested in his work as a priest. He held a number of posts within the Church. At Liverpool he was the first pastor of the famous floating church but, while he was at Bradford where he was vicar, he became interested in the living conditions of the town's factory workers.

Vice Admiral Sir William Clarkson

Captain Cook and the Scoresby's are joined by another significant seaman, Vice Admiral Sir William Clarkson KBE, CMG, RAN. The last of the letters after his name stand for 'Royal Australian Navy' and are used in much the same way as RN for British officers in the Royal Navy. Sir William is regarded as the co-founder of the Royal Australian Navy and, towards the end of his career, he was described as 'without peer in Australian maritime matters'.

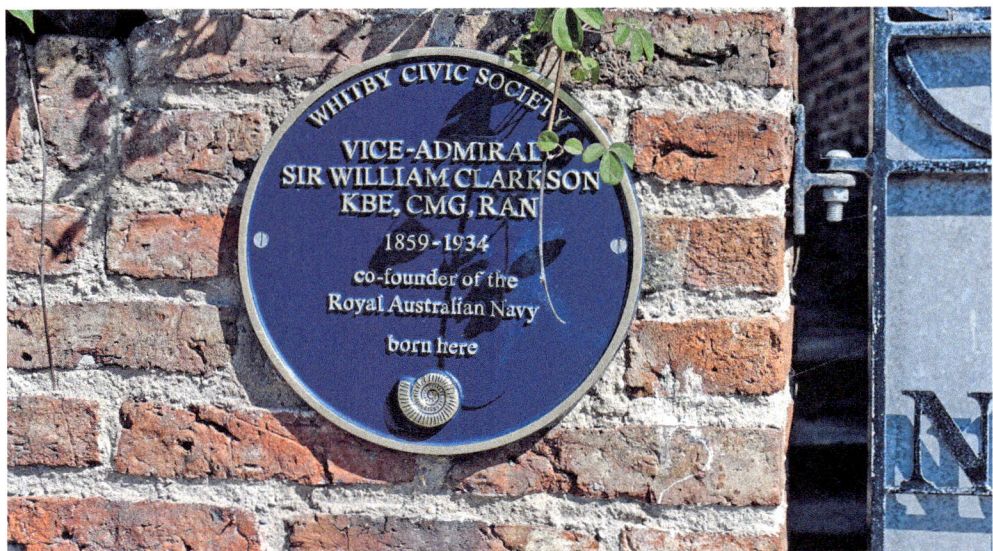

A plaque outside No. 10 St Hilda's Terrace indicates the birthplace of Vice Admiral Sir William Clarkson, co-founder of the Royal Australian Navy.

Sir William was born in 1858 in Whitby, the son of a prosperous draper. He attended a local private school and was articled to the shipbuilding form of Hawthorn's in Newcastle-upon-Tyne where he qualified as a maritime engineer. In 1884 he joined what became the RAN as an engineer lieutenant and was Chief Engineer at the time of the Boxer Rebellion on 1900–01. At this time he transferred to the Commonwealth Naval Forces, becoming engineer commander in 1905.

It was this body which became the RAN and Clarkson, after visiting naval dockyards in Japan, the United States, Canada and Britain, played a major role in establishing the first purpose-built dockyard at Western Point and commissioning the first ships for the Royal Australian Navy. After retirement from the Navy he continued to serve Australia in a number of capacities. It was his wish that, after his death in Australia, in 1934, his remains should be brought back to Whitby where they were interred at St Mary's church.

Four significant maritime lives, and though only one of them was born in Whitby, all of them have left their mark.

From Page to Screen

People have been coming to Whitby 'to take the air' for over 200 hundred years. It is one of our oldest and leading holiday resorts, but visitors are attracted to the town for a number of reasons and it is not only its sea air, though this is famously good and healthy, that brings people to Whitby.

Whitby has the finest natural harbour between the Tyne and the Humber and, those who have been fortunate enough, on a calm and sunny summer's day to sail into Whitby harbour, count this as one of their great life experiences. On the other hand, those who have arrived by sea on a black, stormy sea are less effusive. Locals remind them of Bram Stoker's 'immense dog [which] sprang on deck from below … and running, forward jumped from the bow on to the sand'. The dog of the story, made for the steep East cliff 'where the churchyard hangs over the laneway to the east pier' and 'it disappeared in the darkness'.

So was born the story of Dracula, a story which, as we have seen, still attracts thousands to Whitby every year. Many of these visitors make their way to Tate Hill Beach, the proper name for the expanse of sand and rock, and the rock where the huge dog so dramatically alighted. Many a Whitby sailor, who might normally want to arrive in his home town in a dignified manner, was because of the often perilous the North Sea, glad to land in disarray on Tate Hill Beach and live to tell his tale. It is not for nothing that the sands between the beach and the East Pier became known as Collier's Hope, a final refuge for Whitby's sea-battered coal-carrying vessels of its maritime past.

Stirring stories like these – the famous gothic novel which is read throughout the world, and the rousing stories of Whitby's brave and resourceful sailors – are the catalyst for Whitby's current role as a holiday resort. However, the town, despite its location, has attracted people for centuries; for example, the pilgrims who travelled to visit the shrine of St Hilda.

The Whitby of this time is recreated in Nicola Griffith's *Hild* and though much is made of its remoteness, one gets a real insight into why it was that people, even in these early days, wanted to make their way to Whitby. The arrival of the Vikings was something of a setback but, even to the Norman's, Hilda was such an outstanding individual that another great abbey was founded on the site of her place of worship.

Though never reaching the status of Hilda's time, the Norman abbey attracted people to Whitby. Many of them were traders bringing coal from Newcastle, for instance. At first the monks probably put up their visitors but, such was the volume of business, that local people seized the opportunity to provide services for them, and thus Whitby was born.

There is still enough of this ancient Whitby that has survived to make the town an attractive place to visit. Its narrow streets, winding lanes, old buildings and interesting street names have appealed to writers, artists and photographers. Few towns in England can have such a diverse cultural history! Where else can you see fishermen landing their catches, the workers in a kipper smokery hard at work and the town's many street characters rubbing shoulders?

It is all there in Whitby, even today, just as it was in the past. It might have been difficult for visitors to get to Whitby, except by sea, until the coming of the railways. However, once the railways arrived, in 1836, even though the line from Pickering was single track and the carriages were horse drawn, Whitby quickly became a destination for numerous holiday makers, writers, artists and photographers and has been so, despite what Dr Beeching did to the railways, ever since.

The town, as we have seen, was visited by Bram Stoker and the repercussions of his famous book are still being felt. However, Whitby has attracted other writers with Charles Dickens, Wilkie Collins, Lewis Carol and Elizabeth Gaskell, probably being the best known.

Elizabeth Gaskell

Elizabeth Gaskell, otherwise known as Mrs Gaskell, is known for her novels, *Mary Barton* (1848), *Cranford* (1853) and *North and South* (1855), but she is less well-known for the book in which Whitby plays a part. This novel is entitled *Sylvia's Lovers* (1863) and is a much more romantic

Elizabeth Gaskell.

novel than these earlier works. It is set in Whitby, which Gaskell renames Monkshaven, but the story is not contemporary with the brief visit she made to the town in 1859.

Mrs Gaskell stayed at No. 1 Abbey Terrace on the West Cliff, property that was part of George Hudson's (the 'Railway King'') vision for Whitby, which was never completed. This was at a time when Whitby had ceased to be an industrial centre and was becoming a destination for tourists. The story of the book is based very firmly in the 1790s – days when the town earned its living directly from the sea, when Monkshaven men crewed the colliers, whalers and fishing boats and when industries such as shipbuilding and sailcloth making were still important.

However brief was her stay, Mrs Gaskell did have an appreciation of Whitby's topography. Very early in the book she writes:

> Monkshaven itself was built by the side of the Dee (her name for the Esk), just where the river falls into the German Ocean. The principal streets of the town ran parallel to the stream and smaller lanes branched out of this, and straggled up the sides of the steep hill, between which the river and the houses were pent in. There was a bridge across the Dee, and consequently a Bridge Street running at right angles to the High Street; and on the south side of the stream there were a few houses of more pretention, around which lay gardens and fields. It was on this south side of the town that the local aristocracy lived. And who were the great people of this small town? Not the younger branches of the county families that held hereditary state in their manor-houses on the wild bleak moors, that shut in Monkshaven almost as effectually on the land side as ever the waters did on the sea-board. No; these old families kept aloof from the unsavoury yet adventurous trade which brought wealth to generation after generation of certain families in Monkshaven.

The trade to which Mrs Gaskell refers is whaling. It was as dangerous as it was (or as she put it, 'unsavoury') from the process by which whale blubber was reduced to oil in the melting houses that lined Whitby's river bank. The novel is written at two levels: it is aware of the national context (the French Wars) and what is happening in Monkshaven – the activities of the press gang. *Sylvia's Lovers*, though, as the title implies, is as much about personal relationships as it is about historical events.

The book is still in print and is published in the Penguin Classics series, with an introduction by Shirley Foster. For those lovers of Whitby who have not read it, they should do so. It is sure that they would have done if the book had been entitled, 'Sylvia's Lovers: A Story of Whitby'. That said, not everything in the book about Whitby is factually correct. Those who are knowledgeable about Whitby will spot that, but this does not detract from what many people claim is one of Elizabeth Gaskell's better novels.

However, not everyone agrees. A commentator has written that the book 'represents a sudden lapse into melodrama' which 'reduces and cheapens an interesting story'. That story has not been outlined because the writers of this book did not want to spoil it for future readers. In it there are the two men who were the main character's (Sylvia) lovers. They know each other and one of them exploits an advantage he has over the other – but is duplicity rewarded? There is, as with novels of this kind, a surprising and unpredictable ending. Mrs Gaskell called it, 'The saddest story I ever wrote'.

Charles Dickens

Charles Dickens stayed in Whitby at Mulgrave Castle, which is a few miles out of Whitby. The castle is home of the Marquis and Marchioness of Normanby, whom Dickens counted among his friends. Dickens dedicated his novel *Dombey and Son,* which was published in monthly parts between 1846 and 1848, to the Marchioness.

In the story, the sombreness of the Dombey mansion is contrasted with the warm-heartedness, if not very business-like environment, of the shop of Solomon Gills. It is a device that Dickens used to effect in other novels. Of these *A Christmas Carol* (1843) is the best known and in this instance, Scrooge's miserable counting house is contrasted with the poverty, but simple pleasures, of the home of the Cratchit family.

Right: The famous author, Charles Dickens, stayed at the nearby Mulgrave Castle and was influenced by Whitby and the surrounding area.

Below: The White Horse and Griffin on Church Street was once frequented by Charles Dickens.

There is a connection between these two novels. Although Dickens had visited Whitby as early as 1836, when its famous railway was still under construction, he made the journey to North Yorkshire again in 1844 when he attended the funeral of another friend, Charles Smithson (a lawyer with a practice in Malton).

Dickens had visited the firm's offices in Malton's Chancery Lane on a previous occasion. It is credited as being the inspiration for Scrooge's counting house in *A Christmas Carol,* where the character of Scrooge, emerged from the office as visited by Dickens. Mr Smithson's house was Easthope Hall, near Malton, and when Dickens was there he met the lady who the character Mrs Sarah Gamp is based. She is the alcoholic midwife and nurse in the novel, *Martin Chuzzlewit.*

After the funeral at Malton, Dickens travelled to Lythe as the guest of Lord Normanby at Mulgrave Castle, and while there, Lord Normanby took it upon himself to show Dickens the countryside around Whitby. They are reputed to have enjoyed a meal at the White Horse & Griffin, in Church Street in the town.

These days, the estate of around 15,000 acres at Mulgrave Castle is not normally opened to the public, but it is worthy of our attention because an owner of the building may very well have been involved in one of England's most enduring historical mysteries, one which rivals in interest the disappearance of the Princes in the Tower.

There have been three significant properties at Mulgrave, but there could have been four. The first of these may have been a Roman structure: building materials from that era have been found incorporated into the probable third building on the site that is known as the Old Castle. The ruins of this building are likely to have had Norman origins, but they were slighted on the orders of Parliament after the Civil War in the seventeenth century. There are, apart from ditches and mounds, no substantial remains of the second building there. However, it is thought that it may have been a fort associated with Duke Wada, who lived in the eighth century.

The last building at Mulgrave (potentially the fourth) is the country house which was built by Lady Catherine Darnley, who was the illegitimate daughter of James II and wife of John Sheffield, 1st Duke of Buckingham & Mulgrave. The estate passed to the Phipps family who are still in possession, though it was famously leased to Duleep Singh, the last Maharajah of the Punjab, in 1858.

This diversion came about because Charles Dickens was a visitor to Mulgrave Castle. Dickens was responsible for encouraging his contemporary, and friend, Wilkie Collins to visit Whitby. Collins, though not as highly regarded now as he was in the nineteenth century, was during his lifetime a very successful novelist. He rivalled Dickens for popularity, though the two men were friends and worked together on a number of projects.

Wilkie Collins

Wilki Collins was in Whitby in 1861 when he was accompanied by Caroline Graves, who is thought to have been the inspiration for his novel *The Woman in White*, which had been published the year before. They likely met in 1856 and two years later were living together, something which lasted, almost continuously, until Collins died in 1889.

The reference to Caroline being the inspiration for *The Woman in White* comes, not from Collins himself, but the son of the artist Sir John Everett Millais. In a biography of his father, he describes a melodramatic night-time meeting of Millais, Wilkie Collins and Charles Collins with a distraught woman running away from a man who is keeping her prisoner under mesmeric influence. There is a scene in *The Woman in White* which is reminiscent of this incident.

Lewis Carroll

Another Victorian novelist who knew Whitby quite well (he stayed at No. 5 East Terrace in the town on at least seven occasions) was Lewis Carroll, otherwise known as Charles Lutwidge Dodgson (1832–98). He was an Oxford mathematician but remains famous

Right: Lewis Carroll – was his famous character, Alice, created in Whitby?

Below: The La Rosa Hotel in Whitby was once the holiday home of Lewis Carroll.

as the author of *Alice's Adventures in Wonderland* (1865) and *Through the Looking Glass* (1871). However, it is often not appreciated that his very first publication to see the light of day took place in Whitby. This was a satirical poem entitled 'The Lady of the Ladle', published in the *Whitby Gazette* during Caroll's visit of 1854.

Whitby was probably important to him in several different ways. The poem, the 'Walrus and the Carpenter,' is often thought to have been the product of Carroll's visits to Whitby, but when he was there in 1854, it is likely that he was experimenting with how stories might be told, particularly to children. He used the direct approach when at the beach but, at the same time, he was establishing himself as humorous journalist in the pages of the local newspaper. The 'Walrus and the Carpenter' did not appear until the publication of *Through the Looking Glass* in 1871.

Other Writers

There are a host of other writers who have been inspired by Whitby. There is not room for them all. Apologies to anyone missed out; many of them have linked with Whitby's associations with the paranormal. Robert E. Swindells is one of them. He is a Bradford born former primary school teacher who specialises in the writing of children's and young adult fiction. He was inspired by a school trip to Whitby to write *Room 13*, for which he won the Red House Award. The novel tells the story of a group of young friends who stay at creepy guest house in Whitby.

Robin Jarvis, also a writer of young adult fiction, wrote the *Whitby Witches*, one of a number of novels he has written which are inspired by the town. The *Whitby Witches*, the most well-known of the books, is based on local folklore and the reader gets an instant feel for the kind of place Jarvis is writing about when he states, 'The first time I visited Whitby, I stepped off the train and knew I was somewhere very special'.

This story is about a young brother and sister. They are orphans and are placed in Whitby with an eccentric and elderly spinster, Miss Alice Boston, who adopts them. Miss Boston tells the boy, Ben, scary stories associated with the town. He loves horror stories but he has a sixth sense and can see the spirits of the dead, including those of his late parents. Jennet, Ben's sister, thinks he is making things up with the intention of causing trouble but, then, Ben meets the 'fisher-folk', small humanoids who can only be seen by those who have a sixth sense.

The story has been told well and it is no surprise that it has been popular with young people. The same can be said of the works of G. P. Taylor of which *Shadowmancer* (2002/03) was the first. Like some of Robin Jarvis' books, this one takes place in Whitby, where the book was first put on sale in a privately printed edition.

Mr Taylor was inspired to write books of this kind but approached them from a quite different angle. He was as an Anglican clergyman, concerned to contradict atheist propaganda in children's books. Though some have criticised him for what they regard as his negative portrayal of witches and pagans, the books have been very successful. In fact *Shadowmancer,* which is one of four young people's novels, has been compared to *The Chronicles of Narnia* by C. S. Lewis.

Michel Faber is a Dutch-born Australian, whose book *The Hundred and Ninety-Nine Steps* (2001) has obvious connections with Whitby. In fact, the steps that lead from the town to the ruins of the medieval abbey, act in the story as a link between the twenty-first century and the past.

In the book, Sian, who is concerned about her nightmares, decides to join an archaeological dig that is taking place at Whitby Abbey. What she discovers is not an artefact but a mystery, and a long hidden murder mystery at that. This book is not written for children but it has been described as a historical thriller, a romance and a ghost story all rolled into one.

The abbey at Whitby, the first abbey, that is, features very prominently in a new novel, published in 2014, by a Yorkshire-born writer, Nicola Griffith. It is entitled simply as *Hild* and it takes the reader back to the North East of England in the seventh century, the time when St Hilda of Whitby was one of the leading figures of the age. The book recreates the political, social and religious landscape of the times often identified as the 'dark ages'. This might sound a little daunting, but it should not put off the reader as the book is like a thriller and is another worthy addition to a growing list of novels inspired by Whitby.

The final novel to be mentioned is A. S. Byatt's *Possession: A Romance* (1990), which won the Booker Prize in that year. The novel takes us back to Victorian England and Byatt creates two fictional poets of the time, who it is discovered, may have had an affair. A race begins to uncover the truth when two academics join forces to research the subject. If such a romance can be shown to have taken place it might have far-reaching effects on the career of at least one of the researchers, but the there are other surprising consequences.

The author has Yorkshire connections and Whitby comes into the story because the two fictional Victorian poets spent time there. Byatt recreates the Whitby of those times, when the town was something of an attraction for the literati, but the Whitby of today is just as important. The book was made into a film, starring Gwyneth Paltrow, in 2002.

Whitby, and the area around the town, has served as the backdrop of a number of films. Goathland railway station is used as the location of Hogwart's School Station in J. K. Rowling's *Harry Potter and the Philosopher's Stone* (2001). Another film, *Captain Jack* (1999), was filmed in Whitby. It starred the late Bob Hoskins as the Captain of the title, a Whitby man who wanted to recreate the Artic adventures of 'Captain Scoresby'. Whitby, then, was an ideal place in which to film parts of this film. *Shackleton, the Arctic Explorer*, starring Kenneth Branagh, was shot in 2002 and, this television mini-series was filmed partly in Whitby. The Simply Red music video for 'Holding Back the Years' was shot in Whitby's Church Street and the cover of the single features the lead singer, Mick Hucknall looking out of his harbour window with the lifeboats in the background.

Did you Know?

There is an account of Lewis Carroll's stay at Whitby by one of his companions (a group made up of fellow mathematicians). Dr Thomas Fowler recalled that Carroll used to sit on a rock on the beach, telling stories to a circle of eager young listeners. He believed that this was how, as he put it, 'Alice was incubated', and developed into the main character from *Alice's Adventures in Wonderland* and *Through the Looking Glass*.

Whitby in Sepia

However, we cannot leave Whitby without mentioning a photographer, Frank Meadow Sutcliffe. It is a misnomer to use the phrase 'a photographer' when referring to Mr Sutcliffe. He was a pioneering photographic artist, and he remains, without doubt, *the* photographer of Whitby; his images of the town and its people are famed throughout the world.

Frank Meadows Sutcliffe was not a Whitby man by birth. He was born in Headingley, near Leeds in 1853, just at the time when photography was being developed as an art form. His father, Thomas Sutcliffe, was a water colour artist, etcher and lithographer so Frank was born into an artistic household, though he received only a minimal education at a local dame school.

Frank's first venture into photography was in Tunbridge Wells in Kent, where he ran a small photographic portrait business, but he had ambitions to be more than this and in 1871 he moved to Whitby. At first he lived in the town, at Bloomfield Terrace, and continued with his portrait photography business at his studios in Skinner Street. Later he moved to the nearby village of Sleights, where he married and brought up a family.

When he had the time, he took photographs of ordinary people in Whitby, building up, as he did so, a complete and revealing picture of a Victorian seaside town and the people who lived and worked there. His photographs cover many, if not quite all, aspects of local life: the abbey, the harbour, fisher folk at work and at rest, children at play, street scenes in the town and he took many images of Robin Hood's Bay, Staithes, Runswick and Sandsend.

His work was not without controversy. His most well-known image, *The Water Rats*, which featured naked children at play in a boat, was censured by local church leaders, though it was not, in any way, erotic. There must have been some compensation for Sutcliffe when the Prince of Wales (later to become Edward VII) bought a copy.

Sutcliffe's images of Whitby and the surrounding area make the town possibly the best documented Victorian town in England. While other towns and cities might have good collections of postcard images, Whitby not only has this but also Frank Meadow Sutcliffe's images of the town and its people at home, at work and at play. It is great pity that all towns and villages did not have their own Frank Meadow Sutcliffe!

The list of those from the world of literature and art who are associated with Whitby is longer than we have managed to fit into this book but we hope that including them gives the reader another angle on this most interesting of towns.

Afterword

There is so much about Whitby that is not known to the casual visitor and, unbelievably, to the lifelong resident. At times we, the authors, would often find ourselves peering round yet another metaphorical corner in search of the next secret that was being revealed and it would have been a simple matter to explore these further. But we have left some of the secrets for you, the reader, to discover. There is so much more to Whitby than meets the eye. You just have to know where to look...

Selected Bibliography

Bance, Peter, Sovereign, *Squire & Rebel: Maharajah Duleep Singh and the heirs of a Lost Kingdom*, (Coronet House Publishing, London: 2009).

Barnwell, P. S.; Butler, L. A. S.; Dunn, C. J., 'The Confusion of Conversion: Streanæshalch, Strensall and Whitby and the Northumbrian Church', in Martin Carver's *The Cross Goes North* (York Medieval Press: 2003).

De Givry, Grillot; Locke, J. Courtenay, *Witchcraft: Magic and Alchemy* (Courier Dover Publications, New York: 1931).

Hanson, Neil, *The Custom of the Sea: The Story that Changed British Law* (Doubleday: 1999).

Hugh, Kendall P., *History of the Old Castle of Mulgrave* (Hull: 1948).

Kroebel, C., *Of Myths, Magic, Witches and Saints: Some Aspects of Folklore Represented in Objects in Whitby Museum*, (Whitby Museum Guide).

Porrit, A., *John Metcalf Blind Road Maker* (Halifax Antiquarian Society Pamphlet: 1962).

Sheeran, George, *Medieval Yorkshire Towns* (Edinburgh University Press: 1998).

Thompson, Ian, *Dracula's Whitby* (Amberley Publishing, Stroud: 2012).

Venerabilis Baedae, *Historia ecclesiastica gentis Anglorum*, ed. By Charles Plummer (Oxford: 1896).

Helgason, Guðmundur, http://uboat.net/wwi/boats/index.html (Retrieved 14 May 2015).

SECRET
WHITBY

Ian Thompson & Roger Frost

AMBERLEY

Acknowledgements

This book would not have been possible without the assistance of several people and the authors would like to recognise the contributions of Christiane Kroebel from the Whitby Literary and Philosophical Society; Margot and Joyce for their childhood memories of growing up in Whitby; Ben Abbatt for sharing his family photograph of crab fishing; and anyone else we may have missed out...

First published 2016

Amberley Publishing
The Hill, Stroud
Gloucestershire, GL5 4EP

www.amberley-books.com

Copyright © Ian Thompson & Roger Frost, 2016

The right of Ian Thompson and Roger Frost to be identified as the Authors of this work has been asserted in accordance with the Copyrights, Designs and Patents Act 1988.

ISBN 978 1 4456 5251 1 (print)
ISBN 978 1 4456 5252 8 (ebook)

British Library Cataloguing in Publication Data.
A catalogue record for this book is available from the British Library.

Typesetting by Amberley Publishing.
Printed in Great Britain.